SHORT SALES
2012

FOR

HOMEOWNERS

LANDLORDS

PROFESSIONAL ADVISORS

FEDERAL MAKING HOME AFFORDABLE
FORECLOSURE ALTERNATIVES (HAFA)

BY

DEAN ALLEN KACKLEY, ESQ.

Thank you, Susan.

IMPORTANT NOTICE: The information contained in this book is not intended to serve as legal advice. Nor does it substitute for real estate, financial, tax, bankruptcy, or other professional advice. This book and its author **cannot and do not guarantee results**.

Copies of this book, periodic updates, and forms
in electronic and PDF format may be obtained as available at

www.MortgageBriefing.com

Industry Intelligence for Real Estate Professionals and their Clients

PREFACE

Short sales are not going away. Rarely known ten years ago, dismissed as too much trouble five years ago, today, they dominate many residential real estate markets. It's the life raft for millions of underwater owners.

It's made believers out of every real estate professional I know -- themselves submerged not long ago by the delays, frustration, and sheer weight of unprepared lenders. Since then, both lenders and professionals accepted the inevitable, and improved their systems and attitudes. Still slow, sometimes inexplicable, forever frustrating, lenders and brokers are closing short sales. Lots of them.

The federal Making Home Affordable program started in April 2009 with a simple premise, some might say naïve: Modify problem loans so payments are affordable and sustainable for distressed homeowners. A year later, seeing too many foreclosures and not enough modifications, the government initiated HAFA, Home Affordable Foreclosure Alternatives, which organizes short sales and pays incentives to compliant lenders.

Begun to help homeowners, the federal modification and short sale programs expanded exponentially in June 2012, to include landlords and rental properties up to four units. It also extended expiration to the end of 2013, but the problem will be around for at least another decade.

Values will have to go up, way up, as far up as they came down. In the meantime, millions of properties will change hands. Sellers will walk away without a dollar of equity or, if they pay attention, a dime of liability. It's not a bad deal under the circumstances. Lenders – loan servicers and the elusive impersonal faceless mortgage investors who pull their strings – will take the hit, off-load as much as possible to the government or pension funds or foreign countries or almost anybody else they can find, and survive, or not.

The real estate marketplace is littered with the debris of greedy lenders, mortgage securities dealers, and loan originators, together with complacent or complicit borrowers and their *fiduciary* agents. Passing around blame for the problem won't help, though some accountability would. Still, here's a little advice that will help, from someone who's seen it from all sides.

Relying on the generosity of banks to solve the problem hasn't worked. Just to get their attention has taken new state consumer protection laws, federal Wall Street reform legislation, and the Department of Justice supported by 49 states attorneys general. It's the same mistake we made when we relied on banks to lend responsibly in the first place. Homeowners in distress need to get educated. Then, instead of leaning on banks, they can stand up or push back when needed.

Here's the situation according to the U.S. Treasury Department and my observation:

- Value of equity lost by homeowners -- $171 billion. This is not lost property value, only the portion lost by the homeowner, which amounts to everything before the loan goes underwater.

- Underwater home mortgages -- 11 million. That's 11 million homeowners with no equity hoping desperately for their homes to float on rising fair market values. On the contrary, these are short sales or foreclosures waiting to happen.

- Foreclosure sales – about 60,000 per month. That's three-quarters of a million homes lost in a year, vastly more of which go to lenders than to private buyers.

- Sales by lenders of properties received in foreclosure – about 50,000 per month. This number was higher a year ago, but now has fallen below the number of foreclosure sales. The result increases the institutional (shadow) inventory of unsold properties.

- Short sales – about 25,000 per month. At this rate, it would take 36 years to sell the 11 million homes with underwater mortgages.

Before moving on to details about short sales and their consequences, HAFA coverage recently added or enhanced these features effective June 1, 2012:

- Removed all occupancy requirements.
    - Principal residence *and* rental properties included.
    - One-to-four residential units included.
    - Property must not be condemned, but may be vacant.
    - Seasonal homes occupied or rented periodically excluded.
- Increased payment to subordinate mortgage lien holder to $8,500 from $6,000, at no cost to borrower/seller.
- Pay borrower *or tenant* who must vacate up to $3,000 in relocation assistance.
- Requires all senior and subordinate secured lenders to release borrower/seller from deficiency liability.
- Allows borrower to make full contractual payments to stay current.
- Extends program to begin transactions by December 31, 2013, and close by September 30, 2014.

Homeowners and landlords: If your property is worth less than your mortgage, whether you stay or go, you need the information in this book. Know your choices and their consequences. Do not wait for circumstances or your lender to make the decision for you.

Real estate professionals, if short sales are new or occasional transactions, you need the information in this book to direct clients toward HAFA or traditional options. It can help veterans, too. Give a copy to your clients and prospects.

You already know that it's far more effective to work with well informed sellers and buyers.

For more information about the Making Home Affordable programs, and specifically the Home Affordable Modification Program (HAMP), refer to my book: "Loan Modifications 2012: Essential Guide for Homeowners, Landlords, Professional Advisors." Or contact me for details about my services.

Wishing you peace of mind and a bright future.

Dean Kackley

TABLE OF CONTENTS

CHAPTER 1

KNOW THE PLAYERS

BRIEF INTRODUCTIONS

Knowing the players is part of the game. Allow me briefly to introduce you to those populating the short sale field.

Lender

You chose your lender when you took its money, or your lender chose you when it bought your loan or the right to service it. Let me explain how I use certain terms:

"Lender" means, when I use it, one or more of the following, depending on context. It refers generically to the collective entity on the other side of your loan from you (adversary). Most often, it means the servicer and those represented by the servicer.

"Servicer" means the mortgage company that receives your payments, bundles them together with thousands of others, retains its fee, and passes the remainder along to the investor according to the terms and conditions of their servicing contract. If you miss a payment, its collections department jumps into action. If you want or need mortgage relief, the servicer's loss mitigation department joins the team.

"Loss mitigation" means the servicer's effort to control and reduce its loss on a defaulting loan. It solicits delinquent borrowers, or responds to their initiative, with offers to consider modification of the loan or sale of the property. This department administers the Making Home Affordable programs for participating servicers. Your application for a modification or short sale runs the loss mitigation gauntlet.

"Investor" means the owner of your mortgage and thousands, perhaps tens of thousands like it. A loan consists of the borrower's obligation to pay and, by extension, the recipient's right to receive payment. The recipient "invested" the loan principal with the expectation of receiving a return on its investment (interest).

Investors are passive, having contracted routine tasks to the servicer. Some might have the same name as the servicer, but they have very different functions. They manage huge amounts of other people's money, subject to securities regulations, according to representations and warranties of their investment prospectuses.

Except very rarely, they were not organized to deal with individual mortgages and borrowers. They are more concerned with credit swaps, derivatives, insurance and other hedges against loss and litigation. Further complicating decision making, some mortgages have more than one investor.

"Insurer" means either the private mortgage insurance (PMI) company that insured a high loan-to-value ratio (LTV) loan for an individual borrower, or a financial behemoth like AGI that insured a pool of thousands of loans against risk of default for an investor. Either, or both, adds another more distant layer to the decision making process.

"GSE" means Government Sponsored Enterprise, also known as Fannie Mae and Freddie Mac. After suffering substantial losses, they were placed into conservatorship under the Federal Housing Finance Agency (FHFA) in September 2008. At that time, together they owned or guaranteed about half of the $12 trillion residential mortgage market, easily the biggest investors. If one owns or guarantees your loan, expects its own variation on the Making Home Affordable program.

"Delegated authority" means that the investor has given broad discretion to the servicer for making loss mitigation decisions. Usually, this is good for implementing Making Home Affordable programs.

Real Estate Broker

Whether buying or selling, do not attempt a short sale without the help of a qualified real estate broker. HAFA requires the borrower/seller to list the property for sale with a licensed real estate professional in the community where it's located. Ask whether the individual agent has short sale experience, and experience with your lender. Experience of the supervising broker also helps and might substitute for a less experienced, but qualified and fully engaged agent. At a minimum, everybody needs to understand the differences between a conventional listing and a short sale. Ditto for the selling (buyer's) agent.

Escrow or Closing Agent

Some call them escrow or title companies, others call them attorneys or closing agents, usually depending on geography. They take instructions from all involved in a sale transaction – seller, buyer, seller's (short sale) lender, buyer's (purchase) lender, and real estate brokers and agents. For short sales, they can be instrumental in helping to gather paperwork required by a short sale lender and meeting its requirements.

Often, buyers select the escrow or closing agent after entering the purchase agreement. For short sales, some escrow or closing agents allow sellers to begin earlier, enabling them to start short sale approval, especially for HAFA. Your real estate agent should be able to advise you.

Trustee

"Trustee" or "Attorney" means the lender's representative, which conducts the foreclosure proceeding. In some states, a third-party trustee carries out the notification and foreclosure auction process under a deed of trust according to state statutes. In others, an attorney arranges a judicial foreclosure conducted by a judge. Once foreclosure starts, expect to hear from them. Their involvement in short sales is marginal, except to postpone a foreclosure auction, and then they are critical. They take instructions from your lender. Make sure that your lender communicates effectively.

Others

Buyers and their agents need to understand how short sales differ from conventional transactions. A short sale buyer must be in for the duration. Be prepared for repeated delays. The best offer is the simplest offer. An aggressive price might work with few or no loan conditions. On the other hand, a ridiculous price probably serves only to waste time. Get pre-qualified for financing with a pre-approval letter and proof of down payment. Submit with your offer, and add a brief statement of qualifications, if you like.

Sellers all need to be onboard, ready, willing and able to fully cooperate in meeting the lender's approval requirements. Avoid window shoppers and such contingencies as move-in deadlines, sale of buyer's property, very low down payments, and repairs. When accepting an offer, the buyer's financing terms and qualifications are critical. Accept a lower price before enduring challenging loan terms. Same with property repairs: less is better, none is best. As a general rule about multiple offers, select the one most likely to close. In a short sale, you get nothing, so price doesn't matter to you. On this, you may agree with your lender: get it done the first time.

Landlords as sellers should be conscious of tenants and tenants' rights, usually imposed by state law. HAFA relocation assistance might be available for your tenant, if you run interference. Refer to the appropriate section in this book.

Landlords as buyer also need to be conscious of tenants and tenants' rights. An added wrinkle is federal legislation requiring 90 days notice to vacate after foreclosure. Some states might match the tougher requirements for short sales, so check with an informed professional. Even in short sales, purchasers buy subject to existing leases.

Negotiators may, or may not be professionals who intervene for a fee to negotiate with lenders about short pay-offs, likely more relevant for subordinate than for senior loans. Though logical candidates, some real estate agents might hesitate. The Secure and Fair Enforcement for Mortgage Licensing Act of 2008 (SAFE Act) requires certification of mortgage loan originators, which might extend to any negotiations affecting essential terms of a residential mortgage. Be wary of anyone charging a fee for an unnecessary service, or of someone not properly licensed or certified.

CHAPTER 2

SHORT SALE

THE MIDDLE COURSE

Short sales offer a middle way between keeping a property through modification and losing it through foreclosure. They dominate large segments of the residential real estate marketplace, which has been littered in the past with debris from failed and frustrated transactions. Many underwater owners face years of negative equity, and some are staring down the barrel of impending foreclosure.

A significant influence in the world of distressed mortgages is the federal Making Home Affordable program. Its original purpose was loan modification through the Home Affordable Modification Program (HAMP). It then expanded to incorporate short sales through the Home Affordable Foreclosure Alternatives (HAFA) program. HAFA regulates short sales for participating servicers and lenders. It depends heavily on HAMP principles and, like HAMP, endeavors to become the industry standard.

The next chapter[1] details how to use HAFA to complete a successful short sale and benefit from its incentives. First, in this chapter, some of the broad issues that distressed borrowers face when deciding whether to modify or sell.

---

[1] Chapter 3, *Managing the Short Sale*, page 15.

What Is a Short Sale?

When a lender agrees to accept less than the full amount owed, it's called a "short pay-off." A short sale is a conventional sale that results in a short pay-off when the net proceeds – price minus costs – are less than the loan balance.

The loan to be repaid consists of two parts. The promissory note creates the loan, and the obligation for a borrower to repay it. The security instrument (lien, mortgage, or deed of trust) pledges the property as collateral and gives the lender a contingent interest in the property.

In a short sale, the lender agrees to accept less than the full amount owed, and releases its lien so title passes unencumbered to the buyer. The question remains whether the lender will also release the borrower from the unpaid portion of the loan, from the shortfall or deficiency. If so, the lender forgives the debt, and the borrower owes nothing more. Otherwise, the unpaid portion becomes a personal liability of the borrower, and the lender reserves a right to sue for recovery of the deficiency.

The borrower still owns the property during a short sale and, therefore, is the seller. As the seller, the borrower selects the real estate agent and lists the property for sale. As in any sale of a mortgaged property, the lender must approve the loan pay-off. Historically, the selling price has been sufficient to fully pay the outstanding loan principal, and the lender's approval was routine. The difference between conventional and short sales is the short pay-off and the lender's approval criteria and decision.

Like a loan modification, a short sale is an alternative to foreclosure. Some mistakenly assume that the lender is the seller, which occurs only after a lender acquires the property through foreclosure. This misperception arises understandably from the lender's significant involvement in approving the seller's circumstances and the property's value. Though not a party to the transaction, the lender plays a pivotal role in the success or failure of the sale.

Deficiency

When a loan is not paid in full, as in a short sale, a deficiency results. It's the difference between the amount owed by the borrower and the amount received by the lender.

The lender can forgive the deficiency, or the deficiency might be extinguished by statute. Otherwise, the sale of the property "strips" the loan of its collateral – the lien, mortgage, or deed of trust – and the deficiency becomes an unsecured personal liability. The lender then may sue the individual borrower for the deficient amount. If the lender prevails, the court awards a deficiency judgment.

The importance of ensuring that the lender waives its right to seek a deficiency judgment cannot be over emphasized. This is accomplished by statute in some states, including California. When a lender approves the short sale of a one-to-four unit residential property, the law prohibits the lender from seeking a deficiency judgment. The prohibition applies to senior and subordinate lenders alike.

Otherwise, the lender's waiver is voluntary. To be effective, it must happen before closing the short sale. The waiver must be in writing, typically contained in the lender's approval letter and closing instructions, and often needs to be negotiated. Without it, close at your own risk or cancel the sale. The alternatives are foreclosure, which, in some states, extinguishes the liability; or, bankruptcy to discharge the deficiency liability. Before deciding to close, or not, get qualified professional advice.

NOTE: Foreclosure would not extinguish a secondary junior loan. Talk to a professional about two potential complications: First, whether or not foreclosure in your state extinguishes the debt and, second, if there is a junior loan or lien, whether it could be settled or forgiven in separate negotiations. If all else fails, open deficiencies might be discharged in bankruptcy; consult qualified legal counsel.

The objective – debt forgiveness – can lead also to tax liability, which is covered elsewhere in this book. Exemptions might be available. Consult your professional tax advisor.

Considerations

When advising my clients, I hear several common themes. Significant personal reasons compel homeowners to stay with the property and modify the loan: family, friends, neighborhood, schools, sweat equity, pride of ownership, prospect of regaining lost equity, sentimental and emotional attachments, affordability of a modification, expense of moving and renting, deficiency liability and tax, credit record, a sense of responsibility, and similar considerations.

Others want out. The loan is unaffordable and the lender won't cooperate. The value has declined, equity is long gone, and the lender won't participate by reducing principal. Frustration has led to despair. They want a fresh start, even with damaged credit and spent resources. Knowing that a short sale harms credit much less than a foreclosure, they hope to reenter the market near the bottom, rather than carrying the burden of a house purchased near the top.

Whether you stay or leave, try to set aside emotions and make an objective evaluation of your current circumstances and your short- and long-range goals. You have a choice among modification, short sale, strategic default, or doing nothing. Modification brings your loan current and gives housing affordability, even if you expect to move in a few years and still face a short sale then.

A short sale now might offer several advantages. Especially after declining a modification, some lenders pay incentives for selling rather than proceeding to foreclosure. While awaiting a short sale – or modification – the foreclosure process might continue, but the actual foreclosure sale usually can be postponed, though not until shortly before the auction. Most already delinquent borrowers do not resume loan payments and, after starting foreclosure, many lenders accept nothing less than the entire amount due.

Keep in mind that you are selling your property and must endure a lock box, showings, appointments, finding a professional real estate agent, listing, selling, and qualifying for the short pay-off. Also, re-orient your attitude regarding price. A short sale means that you have no equity, so a higher or lower price doesn't affect you. Find a price that satisfies your lender, and try to get over your loss and what the market has done to the value of your property. A few prefer foreclosure despite the stress and credit impact.

Most lenders do not consider a modification and a short sale simultaneously, though HAFA no longer prohibits it. Personal financial documentation for a modification usually covers what's required for a short sale, making a switch from modification to short sale easier than vice versa. If you can't decide, start with a modification and convert to a short sale. Find a real estate broker with short sale and HAFA experience, and ask your agent for guidance.

Timing might be important because the debt forgiveness tax exemption for purchase loans secured by a borrower's principal residence expires at the end of 2012. It might be reason to begin a short sale sooner than later. Talk with your qualified tax professional about the exemption, whether it will be extended, and how it might affect your decision to sell. Also, ask your real estate agent about closing by the end of the year.

HAFA

The federal Home Affordable Foreclosure Alternatives (HAFA) program consists of guidelines and financial incentives for loan servicers (lenders) and borrowers to encourage a short sale or a deed-in-lieu to avoid foreclosure. Both alternatives reduce the need for potentially lengthy and expensive foreclosure proceedings, while preserving the condition and value of the property. The program began on April 5, 2010.

Significant changes occurred effective June 1, 2012, consistent with expansion and extension of HAMP and other Making Home Affordable programs. HAFA now includes one-to-four unit residential rental properties, which may be vacant, allows relocation assistance for tenants as well as homeowners, and increases the permissible payment to a subordinate mortgage holder to $8,500 from $6,000. Subject to lender discretion, HAFA no longer subjects borrowers to maximum income limits, though financial hardship still must be claimed.

Deed-in-Lieu of Foreclosure

Deed-in-lieu of foreclosure euphemistically referred to as "handing over the keys," for convenience is shortened to deed-in-lieu or simply DIL. Lenders accept a DIL and take title to the property subject to other liens and claims by subordinate lenders, the IRS, local tax assessor, and other creditors. Most prefer foreclosure, which extinguishes all such claims. Otherwise, both HAFA and lenders expect a borrower to clear title of such encumbrances before the transfer.

Deeds-in-lieu are discussed in the HAFA context in the next chapter. Though only a remote possibility, be aware that HAFA theoretically allows lenders to accept a DIL, and then lease-back or sell-back the property to the defaulting owner.

CHAPTER 3

MANAGING THE SHORT SALE

HOME AFFORDABLE FORECLOSURE ALTERNATIVES

The Home Affordable Foreclosure Alternatives (HAFA) program offers an important alternative to default outcomes. The program consists of two possibilities: a short sale that transfers ownership to a buyer, or a deed-in-lieu of foreclosure (DIL) that transfers ownership to the lender. For reasons discussed below, a DIL is rarely used, so this chapter emphasizes the HAFA short sale.

Initiating HAFA

Clearly, the bias of MHA leans toward modification. Lenders must first consider borrowers for HAMP modification before soliciting them for HAFA. If HAMP fails, the lender then must consider a borrower for HAFA. Borrowers may initiate HAFA anytime by informing their lender. To summarize, lenders must consider a borrower's eligibility for HAFA if the borrower:

- Fails to qualify for a trial modification;
- Fails to complete a trial modification;
- Misses two consecutive permanent HAMP modification payments; or
- Requests a short sale.

MHA requires lenders to respond to a borrower's expression of interest within 45 days, and urges them to use HAFA before using their own proprietary short sale programs.

Lenders and HAFA

Within HAFA guidelines, lenders exercise considerable discretion, primarily to accommodate external forces. Variances in state laws and servicing contracts with mortgage investors might result in different outcomes for similar loans. To ensure fairness and all possible consistency, HAFA expects servicers to develop a written HAFA Policy that describes such variances and their resolution.

Here are some of the issues that a servicer's HAFA Policy might cover. It's a good quick summary of issues that a borrower or real estate agent might encounter.

- How to decide an acceptable sales price.
- How to reconcile differences between lender's valuation and the listing price.
- How to determine settlement amounts to satisfy junior loans.
- Who negotiates with junior and other subordinate lien holders.
- Whether and how to consider borrower's income.
- Whether a borrower (seller) may lease-back or re-purchase the property.
- Under what conditions may an occupant continue to occupy the property.
- How to validate occupancy of owner or tenant for relocation assistance.

Servicers must decide how to deal with such issues. Then, together with answers to such issues, they describe their other procedures in a published HAFA Policy, summarized in a HAFA Matrix posted on their website. Some use a standard MHA format that helps to present the information in a uniform way.[2]

Eligibility

If a borrower previously requested HAMP, and the lender received the signed Request for Mortgage Assistance (RMA), HAFA requires no other financial or hardship information. At their discretion, however, servicers may request additional and updated information.

If a borrower not previously considered for HAMP requests a short sale, then the borrower must submit an RMA or Hardship Affidavit, and the listing and purchase agreements when available. Anyone claiming relocation assistance must submit a Dodd-Frank Certification.[3] Despite minimal HAFA requirements, expect most lenders to require other qualifying documentation, which their HAFA Policy matrix or website might outline.

The lender begins by determining the borrower's HAFA eligibility. All HAFA eligibility criteria are included in HAMP, though not all HAMP criteria are required for HAFA. Most notable is the absence of the monthly mortgage

---

[2] A list of lenders and links to their policy statements can be found at: http://www.makinghomeaffordable.gov/for-partners/understanding-guidelines/Pages/HAFAMatrix.aspx

[3] The Dodd–Frank Wall Street Reform and Consumer Protection Act of 2010, named for Sen. Chris Dodd and Rep. Barney Frank, involves broad Wall Street and mortgage reform. It prohibits mortgage loans to anyone convicted of such violations as fraud or money laundering. Signing a Dodd-Frank Certification affirms no such convictions.

payment ratio.[4] HAMP Tier 1 for homeowners requires a pre-modification ratio greater than 31 percent. HAFA eligibility ignores the borrower's income, leaving its consideration to servicer discretion. Again, check your lender's Policy matrix.

Here are specific HAFA eligibility criteria.

1. The mortgage must be a first lien, senior to other loans.
2. The borrower must be delinquent in payments or at imminent risk of default. Loans in foreclosure or bankruptcy are eligible.
3. The real estate must be a "single family property," which HAFA defines as a property consisting of one-to-four residential units.
4. The property may be a principal residence, a rental property, or both.
5. The property must not be condemned, though it may be vacant.
6. The current loan principal balance, excluding late payments and fees, may not exceed:
   - $729,750 for 1 unit
   - $934,200 for 2 units
   - $1,129,250 for 3 units
   - $1,403,400 for 4 units

Evaluation

First, the servicer must find the borrower, loan, and property eligible for HAFA. Then, evaluation begins with the RMA if income is to be considered, or the

---

[4] Monthly mortgage payment ratio equals monthly PITIA divided by gross monthly income. Refer to the author's book, *Loan Modifications and Short Sales: Essential Guide.*

substitute Hardship Affidavit. The servicer may use borrower information completed and verified during HAMP consideration.

If a borrower or tenant wants relocation assistance, then the borrower must submit applicable evidence of occupancy. Also, a tenant must sign the Dodd-Frank Certification, which already is included in the borrower's RMA or Hardship Affidavit. Subject to servicer and mortgage investor demands, income documentation is not required by HAFA, nor is the IRS request for tax information form 4506-T or 4506T-EZ.

Finally, emphasis has shifted away from traditional income-based lending criteria. Until recently, short sale approval, like good lending practice, leaned heavily on proving the borrower's financial qualifications, or in this case financial hardship. Increasingly, attention focuses on market conditions and the sale transaction. HAFA now emphasizes property value, price, and net proceeds. When conflicts arise with the parties to the sale, however, the program still defers to the servicer's authority within its mortgage investor's limits.

This can help to clarify price expectations early, and to reconcile such expectations among the lender, the seller, and the listing agent. Then, the Short Sale Agreement (SSA), discussed below, sets a value. As described in its HAFA Policy, during the marketing phase, the lender periodically re-evaluates the property value and reconciles discrepancies. If it finds that value has declined, then the listing price must be adjusted. On the other hand, after initially agreeing to a listing price, the lender may not insist on increasing it even if market values have risen.

Expect servicers to perform a financial analysis to predict whether the short sale serves the mortgage investor's best interests. Evaluating HAMP modifications involves a complex computer model called the Base Net Present Value (NPV) Model, which projects whether modification or foreclosure yields more benefit *for the investor* (not for the borrower). Servicers must use their own model to predict whether foreclosure yields more benefit than a short sale. So, despite using a different map, the journey still arrives at the same destination: whether or not foreclosure benefits the mortgage investor more.

CAUTION: The question remains: What's in the best interest of the investor, not the borrower? When your lender tells you that it's here to help, remember you are at least second in line. Its fiduciary, contractual, legal duty is to the investor who owns the loan that your lender services. If you are delinquent, then the lender would not be allowed to help you in any way that might compromise the investor's interest in getting paid by you.

Listing Price

One of HAFA's principal features attempts to correct a serious weakness of traditional short sales. Uncommon in the past because of a regularly appreciating real estate market, short sales completed the listing and marketing phases before the lender became involved. Only then did lenders review the purchase agreement and decide an acceptable value. Differences between the sale price and lender's value led to lengthy negotiations and delays. HAFA calls for reconciliation of price and value at the listing stage.

The term "minimum acceptable net proceeds" (minimum net) means the amount a lender expects to receive from the short sale after subtracting all transaction costs. At a borrower's request, the servicer projects results for a short sale, and determines the "minimum net" needed to satisfy the mortgage investor's best interests. The minimum net may be expressed as a percentage of either the market value or listing price of the property. It also may be expressed as a fixed dollar amount, to which projected expenses of the sale can be added to arrive at an acceptable price. HAFA encourages this exchange before or during the listing phase.

Whether expressed as a percentage of value or price or as a fixed amount, the minimum net accounts for transaction expenses. Such expenses include "reasonable and customary real estate transaction costs for the community" where the property is located. An experienced real estate, escrow, title, or closing agent should know. If the servicer underestimates, then make your argument in a documented dispute or escalation. However, the final determination depends on what the servicer or investor is willing to pay.

Borrower Protections

HAFA offers borrowers several forms of protection, including limitation of post-sale liability, suspension of foreclosure sale, and relocation assistance, all addressed in more detail below. Other protections prohibit passing through most sale costs to the borrower, and enable a non-delinquent borrower to maintain an unblemished payment record.

From the total sale proceeds, the lender is expected to pay all fees, commissions, other charges, and out-of-pocket expenses associated with the sale. In addition, the lender pays subordinate mortgage holders a negotiated amount up to $8,500 to settle their loans, usually arranged by the borrower or borrower's agent. Although HAFA does not require, the lender might pay to remove other liens – property tax, HOA, mechanics liens, for example.

NOTE: Regarding federal tax liens, the IRS will issue a certificate of discharge of property (release of tax lien) in short sales because the senior mortgage(s) generally attach to all equity in the property leaving the IRS lien valueless. Refer to Interim Guidance SBSE-05-1010-054 (October 4, 2011) and IRC section 6325(b)(2)(B).

Lenders may not require borrowers to reimburse operational, administrative, and overhead costs incurred while processing a successful short sale; though such costs may be added to the unpaid mortgage balance if the short sale fails. Neither a lender nor a mortgage insurer, which guaranteed payment on a high-LTV loan, may require a payment at closing or a promise to pay (promissory note) after closing.

The agreement by a lender to allow a short sale might require monthly payments until the sale closes. If so, such payments may not exceed 31 percent of the borrower's monthly gross income, which might result in an amount less than the full regular monthly mortgage payment. It is possible for a borrower to remain current up to this point. However, to make the lower or no required payment would result in a derogatory credit report. HAFA allows a borrower to make the full contract payment to stay current and preserve good credit standing, unless mortgage investor guidelines limit short sales to delinquent loans (borrowers).

CAUTION: If a short sale fails, and then goes to foreclosure, the various costs mentioned above may be added to the unpaid principal balance, increasing the deficiency. Debt forgiveness and related tax liability, or potential deficiency liability, also increase.

Release of Liability

Real estate loans consist of two parts: The loan, itself, evidenced by the promissory note, which contains the borrower's promise to repay the money borrowed; and, the collateral evidenced by a written and recorded security instrument – lien, mortgage, or deed of trust – which gives the lender the right to sell the real estate if the borrower fails to repay the loan as agreed. The term "mortgage" may refer to the two parts together, or to the security instrument alone. The term "lien" usually refers only to the collateral interest, which probably secures a related obligation.

Anyone with an interest in the property – owner, lender, or other lien holder – must release their interest, which encumbers or limits ownership in some way, before title passes free-and-clear in a sale to the buyer. However, releasing their interest in the property does not, in itself, release the underlying obligation.

Traditionally, in real estate sales, the lender received the full outstanding loan balance, which satisfied the obligation, and released or removed its lien unconditionally. In a short sale, the lender receives less than the full outstanding loan balance, which leaves a deficiency, and releases its lien subject to the deficiency, which becomes an unsecured personal liability of the borrower.

In the past, a lender might release its security interest in the property, but would not release the promissory note, which could be enforced by suing the borrower and obtaining a deficiency judgment. HAFA endeavors to close this gap by requiring lenders to waive their right to seek a deficiency judgment. Some states require such a waiver by statute. In California, for example, when a lender approves the short sale of a one-to-four unit residential property, it waives any right to pursue the borrower to recover the deficiency.

If others hold a financial interest in the property or a loan affected by the sale – a subordinate lien holder, mechanics lien, property or federal tax lien, for example – the borrower is primarily responsible for obtaining their agreement to allow the sale. A junior lender may receive up to $8,500 from the sale proceeds, at the senior lender's expense, but others might receive nothing unless from the borrower's relocation incentive or the senior lender's benevolence.

Once satisfied, the lien holder releases the lien, which then allows title to pass unencumbered (free-and-clear) to the buyer.

When a second lender agrees to the short sale, it also must agree to the short pay-off and release deficiency liability. It must do so in writing. HAFA doesn't want any forgetfulness or change of heart when everybody arrives at the closing table. It should go without saying, however, that all such agreements must be in writing. Whether it's the senior or junior lender, or a tax or mechanic's lien, get the release in writing. Insist on it.

Neither may a subordinate lien holder – second or junior lender or anyone else – require a contribution from the borrower *or the real estate agent* as a condition for releasing its security interest or for waiving borrower's personal liability. This applies to reduction of real estate commission below six percent, a cash contribution at or before closing, a promissory note or promise to pay after closing, use of relocation assistance funds, or imposition of prohibited fees.

CAUTION: Beware the end run. Lenders may set their minimum net as a percent of the sale price. For example, Ocwen allows eight percent for seller closing costs. After the permissible six percent commission, little is left. The solution falls predictably to the real estate agents.

Suspension of Foreclosure

A servicer must consider a borrower in default for HAFA, before beginning the foreclosure process. After such consideration, however, guidelines defer to the servicer's discretion. Consistent with its HAFA Policy, a servicer may initiate and continue foreclosure during the HAFA process. Actual sale by foreclosure is prohibited while determining a borrower's eligibility or completing a qualified short sale.

Relocation Assistance

An occupant required to vacate a property as the result of a HAFA short sale might be entitled to receive a relocation assistance payment, formerly referred to as an incentive. The property must be the person's principal residence when the HAFA process begins. It applies to borrowers who sell their homes and to tenants of properties sold by their landlords. Whether for themselves or for their tenants, borrowers make the claim and submit proof of residency and a Dodd-Frank Certification.

The amount is $3,000 per transaction, regardless of number of occupants or units. For example, if the homeowner's family must vacant their home, then the entire amount is paid to the seller. If the homeowner occupies a duplex and rents the second unit to a tenant, then each receives $1,500. If all three units of a triplex are rented, then each of the three tenants receives $1,000. If more than one tenant leases the unit, then all share.

The senior lender pays the amount from the sale proceeds at closing for occupants already vacated or by check after occupants surrender the premises and keys. Then MHA reimburses the amount to the lender, effectively eliminating any impact on minimum net or debt forgiveness that might penalize the borrower.

A borrower who receives assistance may pocket the amount, or use it to pay overdue utilities, legal expenses, minor property repairs identified during an inspection, or other such costs. Borrowers may not use any of the amount, however, to release a subordinate mortgage or other lien, or for the lender's transaction costs.

SUGGESTION: A lender might offer more than $3,000. One example, a borrower was found not qualified for a HAMP or proprietary modification, and then was offered a $30,000 incentive to close a short sale rather than proceed to foreclosure. Guidelines don't say whether HAFA permits incentives exceeding the $3,000 relocation assistance. Inquire, first, about relocation assistance and, second, about short sale incentives.

NOTE: Tenants with a legitimate lease might be able to remain through the lease term, or to insist on at least 90 days notice to vacate a property transferred by foreclosure. Refer to Public Law 111-22, Helping Families Save Their Homes Act of 2009 Title VII, Sections 701-704, Protecting Tenants at Foreclosure Act of the Dodd-Frank Wall Street Reform and Consumer Protection Act. The law does not specifically address short sales, which likely are subject to state tenants' rights.

Short Sale Agreement (SSA)

The Short Sale Agreement (SSA) begins a HAFA transaction near the point when the borrower-seller enters a listing agreement. An alternative starting point is after signing a purchase agreement, which a section below explains.[5]

The servicer, on behalf of the mortgage investor, agrees to terms and conditions of a hypothetical sale. The Short Sale Agreement gives the borrower and listing

---

[5] Refer to *Alternative: Start with the Sale Contract*, page 31.

agent a stationary platform from which to market the property and accept an offer. The SSA is an agreement between the lender and the borrower. It's not a sale or purchase agreement, but it clarifies in advance what that agreement – between the borrower as seller and the buyer – must look like.

The SSA path begins when a borrower expresses interest in a short sale, either at the borrower's initiative or in response to the servicer's solicitation. After confirming the borrower's HAFA eligibility, the servicer performs an evaluation. It doesn't use the Base NPV Model, designed specifically for modifications, but probably runs a financial analysis consistent with investor expectations. If the servicer fails to answer the borrower within 45 days, it must send a written status notice with progress updates every 15 days afterward.

Servicers may use the standard MHA Short Sale Agreement form or adapt it to investor limitations, state regulations, and local real estate practice.[6] Nevertheless, at a minimum, the agreement must provide:

- Fixed length of time for the SSA starting on a specific date (SSA Effective Date) and ending not less than 120 days or more than 12 months later.
- Requirement to list the property for sale with a licensed real estate professional in the community where the property is located.
- Real estate commission not to exceed six percent of the sale price.
- Either a listing price or minimum net.
- Acceptable closing (transaction) costs that may be deducted from the gross sale proceeds.

---

[6] Refer to the standard SSA form at
https://www.hmpadmin.com/portal/programs/docs/hafa/shortsaleagreement050112.doc.

- Borrower's permission for servicer to share personal financial information with others necessary to complete the sale and HAFA reporting.

- Clauses to be included in listing and sale agreements about servicer approval, arm's length transaction, prohibition on resale within 90 days, and related cancellation.

- Various closing notifications, including release of borrower from deficiency liability, availability of relocation assistance, settlement of subordinate liens from sale proceeds and release of borrower liability, and professional advice regarding income tax consequences.

- Amount of required monthly mortgage payment during SSA term, if any, not to exceed 31 percent of borrower's monthly gross income.

- Notice that borrower may choose to make full monthly payments to stay current on the loan.

- Servicer's promise not to complete a foreclosure sale during the SSA term.

- Conditions under which the SSA can be terminated.

Accepting the SSA

To accept the SSA, the borrower must sign and return it within 14 days from its effective date, together with a copy of the listing agreement, information about any subordinate liens, and occupancy of the property. In addition to other SSA provisions, the borrower agrees to:

- Provide requested information to verify eligibility.
- Maintain the property and actively market it through the listing broker.

- Work toward clearing subordinate loans, liens, and other impediments to conveying title to a buyer.
- Make monthly payments required by the SSA, if any.
- Prove occupancy for anyone requesting relocation assistance, and provide the Dodd-Frank Certification.

Note: Foreclosure sale must be suspended during the SSA. Failure to make a monthly payment required by the SSA is cause for termination. Termination of the SSA lifts the suspension, and a foreclosure may proceed to sale. It's possible, though unlikely, that missing one or more of the payments could lead to termination; and very unlikely without prior notice. However, MHA guidelines don't describe procedures for SSA termination and subsequent foreclosure, so it's your lender's call.

Request for Approval of Short Sale (RASS)

Another borrower obligation requires submission of a purchase offer within three business days after accepting it, accompanied by another HAFA form, the Request for Approval of Short Sale (RASS).[7]

The following must accompany the form, completed and submitted by either the borrower or listing agent:

---

[7] Use the standard form RASS at
https://www.hmpadmin.com/portal/programs/docs/hafa/requestforapprovalofshortsale050112.doc.

- A copy of the signed purchase offer (sales contract) with all addenda, and one might assume all disclosures and related signed or initialed forms.

- Documentation regarding the buyer's funds (account statement) or loan pre-approval on lender letterhead. Though not stipulated, assume that you will need proof of both down payment *and* loan pre-approval.

- Information about subordinate liens, their status, and progress toward negotiating their release.

Within 10 business days after receiving the RASS and accompanying documentation, the servicer must approve or disapprove. It *must* approve, if the price minus allowable costs equals or exceeds the minimum net, and other terms and conditions of the SSA are met. It *may* approve a lower minimum net. Approval may not be conditioned on reduction in the real estate commission or contributions by the agent or the borrower. The servicer may designate a time frame for closing, but not less than 45 days from the purchase agreement date unless the borrower consents.

SUMMARY: If SSA terms are met, servicer must approve the purchase (sale) agreement, must allow 45 days to close (during which the occupant may stay in the property), may not reduce the real estate commission, and may not ask the real estate agent or the borrower to contribute financially.

Alternative: Start with the Sale Contract

The Alternative Request for Approval of Short Sale (Alt RASS) begins with a signed purchase (sale) agreement, rather than an SSA. Complete and sign the Alt RASS form.[8] Submit it with the following:

- The complete signed agreement with all addenda and attachments.
- Hardship Affidavit or Request for Mortgage Assistance (RMA).
- Evidence of occupancy for residents of the property, and the Dodd-Frank Certification for tenants eligible for relocation assistance.

Servicer then determines borrower's eligibility for HAFA, informs borrower about the availability of HAMP for consideration before selling, and responds to the purchase (sale) agreement. Servicer may approve, disapprove, or condition approval on changes (counter-offer) to the agreement. Approval may not be conditioned on reduction of the real estate commission below six percent.

Response, or explanation of delay, must go to borrower within 45 days after receiving the Alt RASS. Most lenders will alert borrowers about incomplete submissions, but MHA guidelines give no direction, so stay in touch regarding status.

---

[8] Refer to the standard form Alternative RASS at
https://www.hmpadmin.com/portal/programs/docs/hafa/altrass050112.doc.

Deed-in-Lieu of Foreclosure (DIL)

A deed-in-lieu of foreclosure (DIL) transfers property ownership to the lender rather than proceeding to foreclosure on a delinquent loan. It's sometimes referred to as "handing over the keys." HAFA leaves this option to a servicer's discretion consistent with its HAFA Policy and mortgage investor guidelines. To approve a HAFA DIL, the servicer and mortgage investor must release the debt and waive related claims against the borrower. Transfer of title extinguishes the mortgage lien.

Typically, before accepting a deed-in-lieu, servicers expect borrowers to make good faith efforts to list and market a property. Under circumstances agreeable to the investor, HAFA allows servicers to accept a DIL without requiring a marketing period. Most likely, borrower and servicer entered an SSA that expired without a sale. If it included an optional DIL provision, the investor would be obligated to take the deed-in-lieu.

Of potential interest are the following possibilities. If an owner or tenant must vacate on completion of the DIL transaction (closing), the $3,000 relocation assistance may be available. On the other hand, a servicer may allow an owner or tenant to continue occupying the property. HAFA theoretically allows lenders to accept a DIL, and then lease-back (deed-for-lease) the property to the defaulting owner with or without a future buy-back option. Though only a remote possibility, such an arrangement would be included in the DIL Agreement with the servicer and endorsed by the investor. If interested, speak with a supervisor at your lender.

Short Sale versus Modification

A borrower may not participate in a Short Sale Agreement (SSA) and a HAMP Trial Period Plan (TPP) and at the same time, according to MHA guidelines. This suggests that a borrower could list and market the property without an SSA while applying for HAMP, but before TPP approval.

Because MHA guidelines do not specifically endorse the approach, permission probably falls to servicer discretion. The Request for Mortgage Assistance (RMA) asks whether the property is for sale; if yes, it might interfere with your HAMP application. If you try this approach, be sure that your real estate broker is on board, and that the listing agreement allows cancelation on entering a TPP.

Chapter 4

Escalation

Challenging Non-Compliance

Early and persistent failure by some servicers to implement the Making Home Affordable (MHA) program in good faith, forced Treasury to renew efforts aimed at correcting errors, delays, and redundancies by lenders. The process escalates disputes arising primarily from interpretation of guidelines, eligibility decisions, property valuation, notification deadlines, and human error.

Initiated by the borrower or borrower's representative, escalation begins and ends within the servicer's loss mitigation hierarchy, subject to initiative and review of federal MHA personnel. Escalation endeavors to remedy mistakes, ironically, by using the same information that led to the dispute. The servicer alleged to have made the mistake is expected to correct it. Aggrieved borrowers may advocate for themselves, or may call upon third party non-profit or private counselors, according to a defined procedure.

Most important, the rules prohibit foreclosure sales during the escalation process. For modifications, www.CheckMyNPV.com attempts to remove some of the mystery surrounding the most common conflict, the complex Net Present Value (NPV) Test. Many short sale conflicts can be avoided by the Short Sale Agreement (SSA).

Resources

Anyone inquiring about mortgage relief will hear from their lender about a free 24-hour telephone help-line operated by the non-profit Homeownership Preservation Foundation (HPF). The HOPE™ Hotline[9] directs callers to HUD-approved housing counselors, who provide homeowners with free foreclosure prevention information. They are not employees of the Foundation, Housing and Urban Development (HUD), or Making Home Affordable (MHA). They give borrowers a preliminary assessment of their eligibility for MHA programs, and refer them to MHA for detailed program or non-approval questions. Collectively, these resources are called MHA Help, and borrowers access them directly.

Another resource is the HAMP [HAFA] Solution Center (HSC) to manage escalated cases exclusively from housing counselors, government offices, professional advisors, and other third parties acting on behalf of a borrower. More about third party escalation later in this chapter.

Escalated Case

Borrower inquiries and disputes that rise to the level of an "escalated case" usually involve the following issues:

- Whether servicer assessed the borrower for the correct MHA program(s);
- Whether non-approval, or servicer's written explanation, were incorrect; or

---

[9] The HOPE Hotline telephone number is 888-995-HOPE.

- Whether servicer started or continued foreclosure contrary to guidelines.

An escalated case might begin in the federal hierarchy. Then, the HAMP [HAFA] Solution Center (HSC) or MHA Help refers the case to the servicer.

A borrower or authorized third party initiates the case, usually after failing to solicit a satisfactory response to the issues from established loss mitigation contacts. Whoever escalates the case is thereafter called the "requestor." It might refer to the borrower, a non-profit housing counselor, a real estate professional, attorney, elected official or staff, MHA Help, HSC, or Treasury personnel.

Servicers must have written procedures and adequate personnel in place to provide timely and appropriate responses to escalated cases. Hypothetically, with oversight from MHA, servicers decide the outcome, thereby correcting their own mistakes. If the loan and other facts of an inquiry are "substantially similar" to a previously resolved case, however, the servicer may refuse to review it.

Resolution and steps to implement it are communicated within ten day to the borrower and requestor, if different. When HSC or MHA Help concurs with the resolution and the first implementation step occurs, the servicer closes the escalated case.

Third Party Escalation

The world of mortgage relief divides borrowers' representatives into "for-profit" private advisors and "not-for-profit" MHA Help counselors, government representatives, and non-profits sometimes sanctioned by HUD. When authorized by a borrower, any can serve as a requestor. Most servicers refer to them all together as "third party" advocates or representatives, and almost everybody cautions against phonies and scams.[10]

Whether an authorized third party or a borrower advocating for yourself, the following steps apply.

To justify opening an escalated case, introduced in the preceding section, a claim must contend that the servicer did not assess the borrower for the correct MHA program(s) or failed to comply with program guidelines. If you believe that a servicer incorrectly interpreted MHA guidelines, follow these steps:

Step 1: If working through normal contacts and channels at the servicer does not resolve the issue, elevate your concern by asking to speak with a senior manager. Some examples of valid reasons for step 1 escalation arise when the servicer:

- Refuses to stop a scheduled foreclosure sale while evaluating a borrower.
- Charges up-front fees.
- Instructs the borrower to miss a payment.
- Claims that Treasury (MHA) is causing the delay.

---

[10] For identifying characteristics of scams, refer to Appendix 11, *Scam Avoidance*, page 93.

- Advises a borrower to intentionally misrepresent information.
- Claims non-participation when Fannie Mae or Freddie Mac owns your loan.
- Incorrectly denies the borrower's request.

Step 2: If Step 1 does not resolve the issue, then contact the appropriate escalation team:

- If Fannie Mae owns the loan (www.knowyouroptions.com/loanlookup), then call 1-800-7FANNIE(732-6643), or email resource_center@fanniemae.com.
- If Freddie Mac owns the loan (www.FreddieMac.com/MyMortgage), then call 1-800-FREDDIE(373-3343), or email borrower_outreach@freddiemac.com.
- If neither GSE owns the loan, then contact the HAMP Solution Center (HSC) by phone 1-866-939-4469 or email escalations@hmpadmin.com. Property owners, call 888-995-HOPE(4673).

SUGGESTION: Also use these contacts when a servicer incorrectly claims that its mortgage investor does not participate in HAMP, for example, if a GSE (Fannie Moe or Freddie Mac) owns the loan.

To assist a borrower, a counselor must provide written authorization from the borrower to the servicer granting permission to share the borrower's mortgage and personal financial information. Until the escalation team receives written authorization, no information can be disclosed. Standard forms are available or ask the lender. To ensure acceptance, obtain signatures from all borrowers. Ask the lender for specific requirements or its form.

The following is usually sufficient. Also, have it at hand when contacting the servicer.

- Borrower(s) name(s)
- Borrower identification (last four digits of the social security number)
- Property address
- Servicer name
- Servicer loan number
- Third Party name
- Third Party organization
- Third Party email
- Third Party phone
- Third Party relationship to borrower
- Date of most recent (if applicable): Notice of Acceleration, Notice of Default, or scheduled Foreclosure auction

Be aware that signing the Request for Mortgage Assistance (RMA) or the MHA Hardship Affidavit authorizes your servicer to disclose personally identifiable information about eligibility, qualifications, and terms of MHA agreements. Despite having no choice when applying for an MHA program – and even though use of the released information is primarily for statistical and beneficial purposes -- the authorization granted is nevertheless very broad.

Your information may be shared with related mortgage servicers, investors and insurers of both senior and junior mortgages; Treasury, Fannie Mae, Freddie

Mac, and subcontractors in MHA-related roles; and, HUD-approved mortgage counselors.

Be fully informed about the disputed issue. If it involves income and expense numbers or ratios, compare those submitted with any more current and confirm your calculations. If it involves property value, be ready to provide precise comparables, special characteristics, and written documentation. Prepare to overcome the servicer's assumption that it's right and you're wrong. Review the relevant chapters in this book.

Servicer Compliance

Within five business days after receiving an escalated case, the servicer must give the requestor and borrower written acknowledgement of the inquiry with a case reference, a toll-free telephone number for contacting escalation staff, and the Resolution Date. The Resolution Date, by which the servicer decides and communicates the outcome to the requestor and borrower, must be within 30 calendar days after the inquiry. However, failure to comply means only that servicers must provide status then, and update every 15 days afterward until resolution. More like a courtesy than accountability.

Guidelines call for adequate trained staff to manage the escalation case load. Escalation personnel at most major servicers function independently from those who first decided the borrower's eligibility and qualifications. They access relevant borrower documentation directly reducing redundancy. They tend to be knowledgeable about program guidelines, familiar with internal procedures, and empowered with authority to achieve resolution. Borrowers and their authorized representatives are given direct access by telephone and email to escalation staff.

Though written as mandatory requirements, enforcement lacks authority and compliance depends on lenders' willingness and temperament.

Resolution

For each escalated case, escalation staff reviews the information and documentation used by loss mitigation personnel to arrive at the original disputed decision or action. To determine the accuracy of the dispute or inquiry, the analyst may review input values, obtain related property and personal information, recalculate the investor's present value return, and contact the investor directly.

If referred by HSC or MHA Help, then it must concur with the proposed resolution. The borrower or third party advocate needs to be sufficiently familiar with guidelines to validate the outcome.

Suspension of Foreclosure Sale

If a servicer receives an escalated case before midnight of the seventh business day prior to a scheduled foreclosure sale, it must suspend the sale until resolution of the case.

Note: Do not count the foreclosure date. Count back seven *business* days, not including weekends and bank holidays. Submit before midnight of that day: precisely according to your lender's escalation process; and, to the correct office, which might be different than where you previously submitted documentation. Check with your single point of contact relationship manager for details.

The dilemma: When non-approval occurs less than seven business days before the scheduled foreclosure sale, escalate your dispute directly to the HAMP/HAFA Solution Center (HSC) or MHA Help.

If not already in foreclosure, your loan may not be referred to foreclosure until the escalated case is resolved. If already begun, foreclosure proceedings may continue, but the sale may not occur. Actual cancelation of the sale usually happens only after completion of the corrective action, for example, final modification or short sale closing.

The servicer must instruct the attorney or trustee, which actually conducts the foreclosure process, to postpone. This might occur well in advance, but often happens within days or hours before the scheduled sale. Each postponement adds an expense, and some lenders refuse to incur the expense until the last minute. Excessive case loads also delay postponements, adding stress to an already difficult situation.

At this end-stage of foreclosure proceedings, communicate with both the lender and the attorney or trustee conducting the foreclosure. Ensure that instructions have been given *and* received. Otherwise, an unexpected and unwarranted sale might mistakenly take place.

To repeat, so long as an escalated case remains unresolved, the lender may not conduct a foreclosure sale. Nor may a foreclosure conclude while a short sale SSA is active.

If "resolution" brings no change, but your circumstances or the circumstances of your sale change, then communicate immediately with your single point of contact relationship manager. Support it with documentation. If the transaction fails, then revive a back-up offer or describe the strategy that you and your real estate agent will use to expedite another one.

It's easy to become discouraged under such pressure and stress. However, persistence can pay off. Many of my clients after non-approval have escalated or reapplied while under the threat of foreclosure. By responding to every request on time and maintaining a current and complete application file, scheduled foreclosure sales were repeatedly postponed, resulting finally in successful sale.

CHAPTER 5

CONSEQUENCES

Whatever your desired course, if you are in default, attention to the following will improve your outcome. Much applies generally to all MHA programs. Most specifics draw from HAMP guidance, which underlies other Home Affordable programs like HAFA. Otherwise, I've tried to rely on universal legal concepts with some small reference to California where I practice.

Deficiency Liability

Your home or rental property serves as collateral for your real estate loan. You pledged it by giving a security interest to your lender with the right to foreclose if you defaulted on your loan payments. When a loan is not paid in full – short sale, deed-in-lieu, or foreclosure – a deficiency results. Then, when title passes to someone else and you no longer own the property, it no longer secures the loan and any deficiency becomes a personal obligation.

Try to avoid such an outcome. When the property transfers voluntarily in a short sale or by tender of a deed-in-lieu of foreclosure, the lender must consent by releasing its security interest. Terms and conditions are negotiable. Ensure that the lender's consent includes a release of liability and waiver of its right to seek recovery of the deficiency from you personally. If the lender won't agree, then get professional advice and consider withdrawing the transaction and letting the property go to foreclosure.

Ultimately, to collect, the lender would sue the borrower for the deficiency amount. If the lender wins, then the court enters a deficiency judgment, which may be enforced as any other award of the court. Your state foreclosure statutes might release you from deficiency liability by law, or might prohibit the foreclosing lender from commencing a separate lawsuit. State laws vary. Get competent legal advice in the jurisdiction where your property is located.

Some states like California restrict the lender to a "single action," meaning the choice to foreclose is the single or only legal shot at the borrower and extinguishes any further obligation. Because a short sale or deed-in-lieu is negotiated, the "single action" remains, allowing any available collection activities including a lawsuit.

Tax Liability

If a lender waives the deficiency or state law extinguishes it, the debt is forgiven and subject to income taxation. Because lenders now often waive short sale deficiencies, resulting in debt forgiveness, tax liability can be an unexpected consequence, the shadow trailing behind a sense of relief and a new beginning.

The following comes directly from the identified Internal Revenue Service publications, available through the IRS or at www.MortgageBriefing.com. It's general guidance only. **It is not tax or legal advice. Do not rely** solely on what is written here or elsewhere in this book for making decisions that might affect your federal, state, or local income or other tax. State and local laws may differ from federal laws and IRS regulations. Consult your professional financial, tax, or legal advisor.

Principal Residence Exemption (expires December 31, 2012). Normally, forgiven debt results in taxable income. Certain "qualified debt" reduced by mortgage restructuring [modification], or forgiven in connection with a foreclosure might be excluded.[11]

Qualified debt: (1) was used to buy, build or substantially improve the taxpayer's principal residence; (2) was secured by that residence; and (3) did not exceed $2 million ($1 million for a married person filing a separate return). Debt used to refinance qualified debt is also eligible for the exclusion, but only up to the amount of the old mortgage principal, just before the refinancing. [Cash-out or equity loans, therefore, would not qualify.] Source: *IRS Pub. 4705, Mortgage Forgiveness.* See also *IRS Pub. 523, Selling Your Home,* for more information.

Reporting Debt Forgiveness. Borrowers whose debt is reduced or eliminated receive a year-end statement (Form 1099-C) from their lender. Lenders are required to furnish this form to borrowers by January 31. By law, this form must show the amount of debt forgiven and the fair market value of any property given up through foreclosure. [Refer disputes to your lender and, for HAFA, the HAMP Solution Center.] In most cases, eligible homeowners need to report the amount; then, for the exemption, complete and attach Form 982, "Reduction of Tax Attributes Due to Discharge of Indebtedness." Source: *IRS Pub. 4705, Mortgage Forgiveness.*

---

[11] The Mortgage Forgiveness Debt Relief Act of 2007.

Insolvency. Debt forgiven on second homes, rental property, business property, credit cards or car loans does not qualify for the homeowner tax-relief exemption. In some cases, however, other kinds of tax relief, based on insolvency for example, may be available. Source: *IRS Pub. 4705, Mortgage Forgiveness.*

Do not include canceled debt in reported income to the extent that you were insolvent immediately before the cancellation. Source: *IRS Pub. 4681, Canceled Debts, Foreclosures, Repossessions, and Abandonments – for individuals, 2008 returns.*

Here, "insolvent" means that the total of all your liabilities exceeded the fair market value (FMV) of all your assets, meaning the value of everything you own. This includes assets that serve as collateral for debt. It includes exempt assets, which are beyond the reach of your creditors under the law, such as your interest in a pension plan and the value of your retirement account. Source: *IRS Pub. 4681.*

Liabilities include the entire amount of recourse [personal] debts, and the amount of non-recourse [secured] debt that does not exceed the FMV of the property securing such debt. Excluded are debts discharged in Title 11 bankruptcy, and qualified principal residence indebtedness [see above]. Source: *IRS Pub. 4681.*

NOTE: If your primary asset is an underwater home, you have a car loan or lease, and you carry credit card balances, then you might be "insolvent" by IRS standards, despite making ends meet.

Generally, if you exclude canceled debt from income under one of these provisions, you must also reduce your tax attributes (certain credits, losses, and basis of assets). Consult your tax advisor. Source: *IRS Pub. 4681*.

Bankruptcy. Debt canceled in a title 11 bankruptcy case is not included in your income. Source: *IRS Pub. 4681*.

Credit Reporting

Credit reporting for short sales falls into one of two categories, depending on whether the lender forgives the deficiency. When the deficiency is forgiven, the lender reports the loan as "paid in full for less than the full balance." Translation: Though less than the full remaining loan balance at the time of the short sale, the minimum net was accepted by the lender in full satisfaction of the debt. The report shows the account closed with a zero balance and nothing past due. It ends any further reporting on the loan.

When the deficiency is not forgiven, the lender reports the account as "collateral released by creditor with balance owing." Translation: The lender released the lien so clear title could pass to the short sale buyer, but did not waive the deficiency liability. The report continues to show an open account with the same loan, the same account number, and the same original loan amount and date.

Going forward, the lender reports account activity as for any other credit account. The short sale reduced the outstanding balance by the amount of the net sale price, resulting in a new balance equal to the deficiency amount. Other changes depend on agreement between lender and borrower. They might include extending the loan term duration, changing the monthly payment, or forbearing payments or interest for a period of time. The lender reports the original or changed terms, and on-time payments as current or late payments as delinquent. Reporting on the account continues until paid or moved to another status like charged-off, discharged in bankruptcy, or deficiency judgment.

In either case, whether the deficiency is waived or not, any derogatory reports for late payments before closing the short sale will remain on the borrower's credit record.

Needless to say, an open deficiency poses ongoing liability and credit difficulties. A foreclosure might offer an alternative that brings a conclusion to the account and a foundation for healing credit. If the primary senior lender refuses to waive deficiency liability in a short sale, consider cancelling the sale and proceeding to foreclosure. Your decision should consider the foreclosure laws in your state and possible non-extinguishment of a second loan, if any.

Conclusion

A final word about mortgage relief and the consequences of a short sale: Consider more than the liability and credit advantages. Many of my clients initiate a solution to an overwhelming and self-defeating problem, whether it's an unaffordable mortgage or an underwater loan or both.

Some wanted to stay and spent months of anxiety and aggravation feeding the modification monster only to run out of time, patience, and energy. Others turned directly to a short sale as the solution of choice. Either way, these clients have something in common.

They did what property owners do when it's time to leave. They sold. They didn't walk away. They endured a little more pain, regained their sense of self worth, and began to heal mentally, emotionally, and financially.

I recommend it.

Dean Allen Kackley

APPENDICES

> The forms in this section are included only for general reference, and are not intended for reproduction or submission purposes.
> Actual forms can be found at:
> https://www.hmpadmin.com/portal/programs/foreclosure_alternatives.jsp

REQUEST FOR MORTGAGE ASSISTANCE

Making Home Affordable Program
Request For Mortgage Assistance (RMA)

MAKING HOME AFFORDABLE.gov

If you are experiencing a financial hardship and need help, you must complete and submit this form along with other required documentation to be considered for foreclosure prevention options under the Making Home Affordable (MHA) Program. You must provide information about yourself and your intentions to either keep or transition out of your property; a description of the hardship that prevents you from paying your mortgage(s); information about **all** of your income, expenses and financial assets; whether you have declared bankruptcy; and information about the mortgage(s) on your principal residence and other single family real estate that you own. Finally, you will need to return to your loan servicer (1) this completed, signed and dated Request for Mortgage Assistance (RMA), and (2) completed and signed IRS Form 4506-T or 4506T-EZ, and (3) all required income documentation identified in Section 4.

When you sign and date this form, you will make important certifications, representations and agreements, including certifying that all of the information in this RMA is accurate and truthful.

SECTION 1: BORROWER INFORMATION

BORROWER	CO-BORROWER
BORROWER'S NAME	CO-BORROWER'S NAME
SOCIAL SECURITY NUMBER / DATE OF BIRTH (MM/DD/YY)	SOCIAL SECURITY NUMBER / DATE OF BIRTH (MM/DD/YY)
HOME PHONE NUMBER WITH AREA CODE	HOME PHONE NUMBER WITH AREA CODE
CELL OR WORK NUMBER WITH AREA CODE	CELL OR WORK NUMBER WITH AREA CODE
MAILING ADDRESS	MAILING ADDRESS (IF SAME AS BORROWER'S, WRITE "SAME")
EMAIL ADDRESS	EMAIL ADDRESS

Has any borrower filed for bankruptcy? ☐ Chapter 7 ☐ Chapter 13

Filing Date _____ Bankruptcy case number: _____

Has your bankruptcy been discharged? ☐ Yes ☐ No

Is any borrower a servicemember? ☐ Yes ☐ No

Have you recently been deployed away from your principal residence or recently received a permanent change of station order? ☐ Yes ☐ No

How many single family properties other than your principal residence do you and/or any co-borrower(s) own individually, jointly, or with others? _____

Has the mortgage on your principal residence ever had a Home Affordable Modification Program (HAMP) trial period plan or permanent modification? ☐ Yes ☐ No

Has the mortgage on any other property that you or any co-borrower own had a permanent HAMP modification? ☐ Yes ☐ No   If "Yes", how many? _____

Are you or any co-borrower currently in or being considered for a HAMP trial period plan on a property other than your principal residence? ☐ Yes ☐ No

SECTION 2: HARDSHIP AFFIDAVIT

I (We) am/are requesting review under MHA.
I am having difficulty making my monthly payment because of financial difficulties created by (check all that apply):

☐ My household income has been reduced. For example: reduced pay or hours, decline in business or self employment earnings, death, disability or divorce of a borrower or co-borrower.

☐ My monthly debt payments are excessive and I am overextended with my creditors. Debt includes credit cards, home equity or other debt.

☐ My expenses have increased. For example: monthly mortgage payment reset, high medical or health care costs, uninsured losses, increased utilities or property taxes.

☐ My cash reserves, including all liquid assets, are insufficient to maintain my current mortgage payment and cover basic living expenses at the same time.

☐ I am unemployed and (a) I am receiving/will receive unemployment benefits or (b) my unemployment benefits ended less than 6 months ago.

Other:

Explanation (continue on a separate sheet of paper if necessary):

SECTION 3: PRINCIPAL RESIDENCE INFORMATION

(This section is required even if you are not seeking mortgage assistance on your principal residence.)

I am requesting mortgage assistance with my principal residence ☐ Yes ☐ No

If "yes", I want to: ☐ Keep the property ☐ Sell the property

Property Address _____ Loan I.D. Number _____

Other mortgages or liens on the property? ☐ Yes ☐ No Lien Holder / Servicer Name: _____ Loan I.D. Number _____

Do you have condominium or homeowner association (HOA) fees? ☐ Yes ☐ No If "Yes", Monthly Fee $_____ Are fees paid current? ☐ Yes ☐ No

Name and address that fees are paid to _____

Does your mortgage payment include taxes and insurance? ☐ Yes ☐ No If "No", are the taxes and insurance paid current? ☐ Yes ☐ No

Annual Homeowner's Insurance $_____

Is the property listed for sale? ☐ Yes ☐ No If "Yes", Listing Agent's Name _____ Phone Number _____

List date? _____ Have you received a purchase offer? ☐ Yes ☐ No Amount of Offer $_____ Closing Date: _____

Complete this section ONLY if you are requesting mortgage assistance with a property that is not your principal residence.

Principal residence servicer name _____ Principal residence servicer phone number _____

Is the mortgage on your principal residence paid? ☐ Yes ☐ No If "No", number of months your payment is past due (if known): _____

SECTION 4: COMBINED INCOME AND EXPENSE OF BORROWER AND CO-BORROWER

Monthly Household Income		Monthly Household Expenses/Debt (*Principal Residence Expense Only)		Household Assets	
Monthly Gross wages	$	First Mortgage Principal & Interest Payment*	$	Checking Account(s)	$
Overtime	$	Second Mortgage Principal & Interest Payment*	$	Checking Account(s)	$
Self employment Income	$	Homeowner's Ins. rance*	$	Savings / Money Market	$
Unemployment Income	$	Property Taxes*	$	CDs	$
Untaxed Social Security / SSDI	$	HOA/Condo Fees*	$	Stocks / Bonds	$
Food Stamps/Welfare	$	Credit Cards/Installment debt (total min. paymen.)	$	Other Cash on Hand	$
Taxable Social Security or retirement income	$	Child Support / Alimony	$		
Chile Support / Alimony**	$	Car Payments	$		
Tips, commissions, bonus and overtime	$	Mortgage Payments other properties****	$		
Gross Rents Received ***	$	Other	$	Value of all Real Estate except principal residence	$
Other	$			Other	$
Total (Gross income)	$	Total Debt/Expenses	$	Total Assets	$

** Alimony, child support or separate maintenance income need not be disclosed if you do not choose to have it considered for repaying your mortgage debt.

*** Include rental income received from all properties you own EXCEPT a property for which you are seeking mortgage assistance in Section 6.

**** Include mortgage payments on all properties you own EXCEPT your principal residence and the property for which you are seeking mortgage assistance in Section 6.

56

Required Income Documentation
(Your servicer may request additional documentation to complete your evaluation for MHA)

All Borrowers	☐ Include a signed IRS Form 4506-T or 4506T-EZ
☐ Do you earn a wage? Borrower Hire Date (MM/DD/YY) _____ Co-borrower Hire Date (MM/DD/YY) _____	☐ For each borrower who is a salaried employee or hourly wage earner, provide the most recent pay stub(s) that reflects at least 30 days of year-to-date income.
☐ Are you self-employed?	☐ Provide your most recent signed and dated quarterly or year-to-date profit and loss statement
☐ Do you receive tips, commissions, bonuses, housing allowance or overtime?	☐ Describe the type of income, how frequently you receive the income and third party documentation describing the income (e.g. employment contracts or printouts documenting tip income)
☐ Do you receive social security, disability, death benefits, pension, public assistance or adoption assistance?	☐ Provide documentation showing the amount and frequency of the benefits, such as letters, exhibits, disability policy or benefits statement from the provider and receipt of payment (such as two most recent bank statements or deposit advices)
☐ Do you receive alimony, child support, or separation maintenance payments?	☐ Provide a copy of the divorce decree, separation agreement, or other written legal agreement filed with the court that states the amount of the payments and the period of time that you are entitled to receive them. AND ☐ Copies of your two most recent bank statements or deposit advices showing you have received payment **Notice: Alimony, child support or separate maintenance income need not be disclosed if you do not choose to have it considered for repaying your mortgage debt.**
☐ Do you have income from rental properties that are not your principal residence?	☐ Provide your most recent Federal Tax return with all schedules, including Schedule E ☐ If rental income is not reported on Schedule E, provide a copy of the current lease agreement with bank statements showing deposit of rent checks.

SECTION 5: OTHER PROPERTIES OWNED
You must provide information about each property owned other than your principal residence and complete the requested information for each property in this section. (Use additional sheets if necessary)

Other Property #1

Property Address _____ Loan ID Number _____

Servicer Name _____ Mortgage Balance $ _____ Current Value $ _____

Property is: ☐ Vacant ☐ Second or seasonal home ☐ Rented   Gross Monthly Rent $ _____   Monthly mortgage payment* $ _____

Other Property #2

Property Address _____ Loan ID Number _____

Servicer Name _____ Mortgage Balance $ _____ Current Value $ _____

Property is: ☐ Vacant ☐ Second or seasonal home ☐ Rented   Gross Monthly Rent $ _____   Monthly mortgage payment* $ _____

Other Property #3

Property Address _____ Loan ID Number _____

Servicer Name _____ Mortgage Balance $ _____ Current Value $ _____

Property is: ☐ Vacant ☐ Second or seasonal home ☐ Rented   Gross Monthly Rent $ _____   Monthly mortgage payment* $ _____

* The amount of the monthly payment made to your lender – including, if applicable, monthly principal, interest, real property taxes and insurance premiums..

SECTION 6: OTHER PROPERTY FOR WHICH ASSISTANCE IS REQUESTED
(Complete this section ONLY if you are requesting mortgage assistance with a property that is not your principal residence)

I am requesting mortgage assistance with a rental property. ☐ Yes ☐ No

I am requesting mortgage assistance with a second or seasonal home. ☐ Yes ☐ No

If "Yes" to either, I want to: ☐ Keep the property ☐ Sell the property

Property Address _____ Loan I.D. Number _____

Do you have a second mortgage on the property ☐ Yes ☐ No If "Yes", Servicer Name: _____ Loan I.D. Number: _____

Do you have condominium or homeowner association (HOA) fees? ☐ Yes ☐ No If "Yes", Monthly Fee $ _____ Are HOA fees paid current? ☐ Yes ☐ No

Name and address that fees are paid to: _____

Does your mortgage payment include taxes and insurance? ☐ Yes ☐ No If "No", are the taxes and insurance paid current? ☐ Yes ☐ No

Annual Homeowner's Insurance $ _____ Annual Property Taxes $ _____

If requesting assistance with a rental property, property is currently   ☐ Vacant and available for rent

☐ Occupied without rent by your legal dependent, parent or grandparent as their principal residence

☐ Occupied by a tenant as their principal residence.

☐ Other _____

If rental property is occupied by a tenant: Term of lease / occupancy ___/___/___ – ___/___/___ Gross Monthly Rent $ _____
(MM / DD / YYYY   MM / DD / YYYY)

If rental property is vacant, describe efforts to rent property _____

If applicable, describe relationship of and duration of non-rent paying occupant of rental property _____

Is the property for sale? ☐ Yes ☐ No If "Yes", Listing Agent's Name _____ Phone Number _____

List date? _____ Have you received a purchase offer? ☐ Yes ☐ No Amount of Offer $ _____ Closing Date _____

RENTAL PROPERTY CERTIFICATION
(You must complete this certification if you are requesting a mortgage modification with respect to a rental property.)

☐ By checking this box and initialing below, I am requesting a mortgage modification under M.A with respect to the rental property described in this Section 6 and I hereby certify under penalty of perjury that each of the following statements is true and correct with respect to that property.

1. I intend to rent the property to a tenant or tenants for at least five years following the effective date of my mortgage modification. I understand that the servicer, the U.S. Department of the Treasury, or their respective agents may ask me to provide evidence of my intention to rent the property during such time. I further understand that such evidence must show that I used reasonable efforts to rent the property to a tenant or tenants on a year-round basis, if the property is or becomes vacant during such five-year period.

   Note: The term "reasonable efforts" includes, without limitation, advertising the property for rent in local newspapers, websites or other commonly used forms of written or electronic media, and/or engaging a real estate or other professional to assist in renting the property, in either case, at or below market rent.

2. The property is not my secondary residence and I do not intend to use the property as a secondary residence for at least five years following the effective date of my mortgage modification. I understand that if I do use the property as a secondary residence during such five-year period, my use of the property may be considered to be inconsistent with the certifications I have made herein.

   Note: The term "secondary residence" includes, without limitation, a second home, vacation home or other type of residence that I personally use or occupy on a part-time, seasonal or other basis.

3. I do not own more than five (5) single-family homes (i.e., one-to-four unit properties) (exclusive of my principal residence).

Notwithstanding the foregoing certifications, I may at any time sell the property, occupy it as my principal residence, or permit my legal dependent, parent or grandparent to occupy it as their principal residence with no rent charged or collected, none of which will be considered to be inconsistent with the certifications made herein.

This certification is effective on the earlier of the date listed below or the date the RMA is received by your servicer.

Initials: Borrower _____ Co-borrower _____

The following information is requested by the federal government in accordance with the Dodd-Frank Wall Street Reform and Consumer Protection Act (Pub. L. 111-203). **You are required to furnish this information.** The law provides that no person shall be eligible to begin receiving assistance from the Making Home Affordable Program, authorized under the Emergency Economic Stabilization Act of 2008 (12 U.S.C. 5201 et seq.), or any other mortgage assistance program authorized or funded by that Act, if such person, in connection with a mortgage or real estate transaction, has been convicted, within the last 10 years, of any one of the following: (A) felony larceny, theft, fraud, or forgery, (B) money laundering or (C) tax evasion.

I/we certify under penalty of perjury that I/we have not been convicted within the last 10 years of any one of the following in connection with a mortgage or real estate transaction:

    (a) felony larceny, theft, fraud, or forgery,
    (b) money laundering or
    (c) tax evasion.

I/we understand that the servicer, the U.S. Department of the Treasury, or their respective agents may investigate the accuracy of my statements by performing routine background checks, including automated searches of federal, state and county databases, to confirm that I/we have not been convicted of such crimes. I/we also understand that knowingly submitting false information may violate Federal law. This certification is effective on the earlier of the date listed below or the date this RMA is received by your servicer.

The following information is requested by the federal government in order to monitor compliance with federal statutes that prohibit discrimination in housing. **You are not required to furnish this information, but are encouraged to do so. The law provides that a lender or servicer may not discriminate either on the basis of this information, or on whether you choose to furnish it.** If you furnish the information, please provide both ethnicity and race. For race, you may check more than one designation. If you do not furnish ethnicity, race, or sex, the lender or servicer is required to note the information on the basis of visual observation or surname if you have made this request for a loan modification in person. **If you do not wish to furnish the information, please check the box below.**

BORROWER ☐ I do not wish to furnish this information		CO-BORROWER ☐ I do not wish to furnish this information
Ethnicity: ☐ Hispanic or Latino		Ethnicity: ☐ Hispanic or Latino
☐ Not Hispanic or Latino		☐ Not Hispanic or Latino
Race: ☐ American Indian or Alaska Native		Race: ☐ American Indian or Alaska Native
☐ Asian		☐ Asian
☐ Black or African American		☐ Black or African American
☐ Native Hawaiian or Other Pacific Islander		☐ Native Hawaiian or Other Pacific Islander
☐ White		☐ White
Sex: ☐ Female		Sex: ☐ Female
☐ Male		☐ Male

To be completed by Interviewer		Name/Address of Interviewer's Employer
This request was taken by:	Interviewer's Name (print or type) & ID Number	
☐ Face-to-face Interview		
☐ Mail	Interviewer's Signature Date	
☐ Telephone		
☐ Internet	Interviewer's Phone Number (include area code)	

SECTION 9: BORROWER AND CO-BORROWER ACKNOWLEDGEMENT AND AGREEMENT

1. I certify that all of the information in this RMA is truthful and the hardship(s) identified above has contributed to submission of this request for mortgage relief.

2. I understand and acknowledge that the Servicer, the U.S. Department of the Treasury, the owner or guarantor of my mortgage loan, or their respective agents may investigate the accuracy of my statements, may require me to provide additional supporting documentation and that knowingly submitting false information may violate Federal and other applicable law.

3. I authorize and give permission to the Servicer, the U.S. Department of the Treasury, and their respective agents, to assemble and use a current consumer report on all borrowers obligated on the loan, to investigate each borrower's eligibility for MHA and the accuracy of my statements and any documentation that I provide in connection with my request for assistance. I understand that these consumer reports may include, without limitation, a credit report, and be assembled and used at any point during the application process to assess each borrower's eligibility thereafter.

4. I understand that if I have intentionally defaulted on my existing mortgage, engaged in fraud or if it is determined that any of my statements or any information contained in the documentation that I provide are materially false and that I was ineligible for assistance under MHA, the Servicer, the U.S. Department of the Treasury, or their respective agents may terminate my participation in MHA, including any right to future benefits and incentives that otherwise would have been available under the program, and also may seek other remedies available at law and in equity, such as recouping any benefits or incentives previously received.

5. I certify that any property for which I am requesting assistance is a habitable residential property that is not subject to a condemnation notice.

6. I certify that I am willing to provide all requested documents and to respond to all Servicer communications in a timely manner. I understand that time is of the essence.

7. I understand that the Servicer will use the information I provide to evaluate my eligibility for available relief options and foreclosure alternatives, but the Servicer is not obligated to offer me assistance based solely on the representations in this document or other documentation submitted in connection with my request.

8. I am willing to commit to credit counseling if it is determined that my financial hardship is related to excessive debt.

9. If I am eligible for assistance under MHA, and I accept and agree to all terms of an MHA notice, plan, or agreement, I also agree that the terms of this Acknowledgment and Agreement are incorporated into such notice, plan, or agreement by reference as if set forth therein in full. My first timely payment, if required, following my servicer's determination and notification of my eligibility or prequalification for MHA assistance will serve as my acceptance of the terms set forth in the notice, plan, or agreement sent to me.

10. I understand that my Servicer will collect and record personal information that I submit in this RMA and during the evaluation process, including, but not limited to, my name, address, telephone number, social security number, credit score, income, payment history, government monitoring information, and information about my account balances and activity. I understand and consent to the Servicer's disclosure of my personal information and the terms of any MHA notice, plan or agreement to the U.S. Department of the Treasury and its agents, Fannie Mae and Freddie Mac in connection with their responsibilities under MHA, companies that perform support services in conjunction with MHA, any investor, insurer, guarantor, or servicer that owns, insures, guarantees, or services my first lien or subordinate lien (if applicable) mortgage loan(s) and to any HUD-certified housing counselor.

11. I consent to being contacted concerning this request for mortgage assistance at any e-mail address or cellular or mobile telephone number I have provided to the Servicer. This includes text messages and telephone calls to my cellular or mobile telephone.

The undersigned certifies under penalty of perjury that all statements in this document are true and correct.

Borrower Signature	Social Security Number	Date of Birth	Date
Co-borrower Signature	Social Security Number	Date of Birth	Date

09/30/2012

60

HOMEOWNER'S HOTLINE

If you have questions about this document or the Making Home Affordable Program, please call your servicer.
If you have questions about the program that your servicer cannot answer or need further counseling, you can call the Homeowner's HOPE™ Hotline at 1-888-995-HOPE (4673).

The Hotline can help with questions about the program and offers free HUD-certified counseling services in English and Spanish.

NOTICE TO BORROWERS

Be advised that by signing this document you understand that any documents and information you submit to your servicer in connection with the Making Home Affordable Program are under penalty of perjury. Any misstatement of material fact made in the completion of these documents including but not limited to misstatement regarding your occupancy of your property, hardship circumstances, and/or income, expenses, or assets will subject you to potential criminal investigation and prosecution for the following crimes: perjury, false statements, mail fraud, and wire fraud. The information contained in these documents is subject to examination and verification. Any potential misrepresentation will be referred to the appropriate law enforcement authority for investigation and prosecution. By signing this document you certify, represent and agree that: "Under penalty of perjury, all documents and information I have provided to my Servicer in connection with the Making Home Affordable Program, including the documents and information regarding my eligibility for the program, are true and correct."

If you are aware of fraud, waste, abuse, mismanagement or misrepresentations affiliated with the Troubled Asset Relief Program, please contact the SIGTARP Hotline by calling 1-877-SIG-2009 (toll-free), 202-622-4559 (fax), or www.sigtarp.gov and provide them with your name, our name as your servicer, your property address, loan number and the reason for escalation. Mail can be sent to Hotline Office of the Special Inspector General for Troubled Asset Relief Program, 1801 L St. NW, Washington, DC 20220.

Beware of Foreclosure Rescue Scams. Help is FREE!

- There is never a fee to get assistance or information about the Making Home Affordable Program from your lender or a HUD-approved housing counselor.
- Beware of any person or organization that asks you to pay a fee in exchange for housing counseling services or modification of a delinquent loan.
- Beware of anyone who says they can "save" your home if you sign or transfer over the deed to your house. Do not sign over the deed to your property to any organization or individual unless you are working directly with your mortgage company to forgive your debt.
- Never make your mortgage payments to anyone other than your mortgage company without their approval.

08/30/2012

MHA HARDSHIP AFFIDAVIT

Making Home Affordable Program
Hardship Affidavit

MAKING HOME AFFORDABLE.GOV

| HARDSHIP AFFIDAVIT page 1 | COMPLETE ALL THREE PAGES OF THIS FORM |

▶ Loan I.D. Number_____ ▶ Servicer _____

BORROWER	CO-BORROWER
Borrower's name	Co-borrower's name
Social Security Number	Social Security Number

Property address (include city, state and zip):			
I want to:	☐ Keep the Property	☐ Sell the Property	
The property is my:	☐ Principal Residence	☐ Second Home / Seasonal Rental	☐ Year-Round Rental
The property is:	☐ Owner Occupied	☐ Tenant Occupied	☐ Vacant ☐ Other _____

HARDSHIP AFFIDAVIT

I (We) am/are requesting review under the Making Home Affordable (MHA) Program.
I am having difficulty making my monthly payment because of financial difficulties created by (check all that apply):

☐ My household income has been reduced. For example: reduced pay or hours, decline in business earnings, death, disability or divorce of a borrower or co-borrower.

☐ My monthly debt payments are excessive and I am overextended with my creditors. Debt includes credit cards, home equity or other debt.

☐ My expenses have increased. For example: monthly mortgage payment reset, high medical or health care costs, uninsured losses, increased utilities or property taxes.

☐ My cash reserves, including all liquid assets, are insufficient to maintain my current mortgage payment and cover basic living expenses at the same time.

☐ I am unemployed and (a) I am receiving/will receive unemployment benefits or (b) my unemployment benefits ended less than 6 months ago.

☐ Other:

Explanation (continue on back of page 3 if necessary): _____
_____

Have you filed for bankruptcy? ☐Yes ☐No   If yes: ☐ Chapter 7 ☐ Chapter 13   Filing Date:_____
Has your bankruptcy been discharged? ☐Yes ☐No   Bankruptcy case number _____

How many single-family properties, other than your personal residence, do you and/or your co-borrower(s) own individually, jointly, or with others? _____

Has the mortgage on your principle residence ever had a Home Affordable Modification Program (HAMP) trial-period plan or permanent modification?   ☐Yes ☐ No

Has the mortgage or any other property that you or any co-borrower own had a permanent HAMP modification? ☐ Yes ☐ No If "Yes", how many? _____

DODD-FRANK CERTIFICATION

The following information is requested by the federal government in accordance with the Dodd-Frank Wall Street Reform and Consumer Protection Act (Pub. L. 111-203). **You are required to furnish this information.** The law provides that no person shall be eligible to begin receiving assistance from the Making Home Affordable Program, authorized under the Emergency Economic Stabilization Act of 2008 (12 U.S.C. 5201 et seq.), or any other mortgage assistance program authorized or funded by that Act, if such person, in connection with a mortgage or real estate transaction, has been convicted, within the last 10 years, of any one of the following: (A) felony larceny, theft, fraud, or forgery, (B) money laundering or (C) tax evasion.

I/we certify under penalty of perjury that I/we have not been convicted within the last 10 years of any one of the following in connection with a mortgage or real estate transaction:

    (a) felony larceny, theft, fraud, or forgery,
    (b) money laundering or
    (c) tax evasion.

I/we understand that the servicer, the U.S. Department of the Treasury, or their respective agents may investigate the accuracy of my statements by performing routine background checks, including automated searches of federal, state and county databases, to confirm that I/we have not been convicted of such crimes. I/we also understand that knowingly submitting false information may violate Federal law.

This certification is effective on the earlier of the date listed below or the date this hardship affidavit is received by your servicer.

page 1 of 3▶

RENTAL PROPERTY CERTIFICATION

You must complete this certification if you are requesting a mortgage modification with respect to a rental property.

☐ By checking this box and initialing below, I am requesting a mortgage modification under MHA with respect to the rental property having the address set forth above and I hereby certify under penalty of perjury that each of the following statements is true and correct with respect to that property:

1. I intend to rent the property to a tenant or tenants for at least five years following the effective date of my mortgage modification. I understand that the servicer, the U.S. Department of the Treasury, or their respective agents may ask me to provide evidence of my intention to rent the property during such time. I further understand that such evidence must show that I used reasonable efforts to rent the property to a tenant or tenants on a year-round basis, if the property is or becomes vacant during such five-year period.

Note: The term "reasonable efforts" includes, without limitation, advertising the property for rent in local newspapers, websites or other commonly used forms of written or electronic media, and/or engaging a real estate or other professional to assist in renting the property, in either case, at or below market rent.

2. The property is not my secondary residence and I do not intend to use the property as a secondary residence for at least five years following the effective date of my mortgage modification. I understand that if I do use the property as a secondary residence during such five-year period, my use of the property may be considered to be inconsistent with the certifications I have made herein.

Note: The term "secondary residence" includes, without limitation, a second home, vacation home or other type of residence that I personally use or occupy on a part-time, seasonal or other basis.

3. I do not own more than five (5) single-family homes (i.e., one-to-four unit properties) (exclusive of my principal residence).

<u>Notwithstanding the foregoing certifications, I may at any time sell the property, occupy it as my principal residence, or permit my legal dependent, parent or grandparent to occupy it as their principal residence with no rent charged or collected, none of which will be considered to be inconsistent with the certifications made herein.</u>

This certification is effective on the earlier of the date listed below or the date the Hardship Affidavit is received by your servicer.

Initials: Borrower _____   Co-borrower _____

INFORMATION FOR GOVERNMENT MONITORING PURPOSES

The following information is requested by the federal government in order to monitor compliance with federal statutes that prohibit discrimination in housing. You are not required to furnish this information, but are encouraged to do so. The law provides that a lender or servicer may not discriminate either on the basis of this information, or on whether you choose to furnish it. If you furnish the information, please provide both ethnicity and race. For race, you may check more than one designation. If you do not furnish ethnicity, race, or sex, the lender or servicer is required to note the information on the basis of visual observation or surname if you have made this request for a loan modification in person. If you do not wish to furnish the information, please check the box below.

BORROWER	☐ I do not wish to furnish this information	CO-BORROWER	☐ I do not wish to furnish this information
Ethnicity:	☐ Hispanic or Latino ☐ Not Hispanic or Latino	*Ethnicity:*	☐ Hispanic or Latino ☐ Not Hispanic or Latino
Race:	☐ American Indian or Alaska Native ☐ Asian ☐ Black or African American ☐ Native Hawaiian or Other Pacific Islander ☐ White	*Race:*	☐ American Indian or Alaska Native ☐ Asian ☐ Black or African American ☐ Native Hawaiian or Other Pacific Islander ☐ White
Sex:	☐ Female ☐ Male	*Sex:*	☐ Female ☐ Male

To be completed by interviewer		Name/Address of Interviewer's Employer
This request was taken by: ☐ Face-to-face interview ☐ Mail ☐ Telephone ☐ Internet	Interviewer's Name (print or type) & ID Number Interviewer's Signature Date Interviewer's Phone Number (include area code)	

ACKNOWLEDGEMENT AND AGREEMENT

1. That all of the information in this document is truthful and the event(s) identified on page 1 is/are the reason that I need to request a modification or forbearance of the terms of my mortgage loan, short sale or deed-in-lieu of foreclosure.

2. I understand and acknowledge that the Servicer, the U.S. Department of the Treasury, the owner or guarantor of my mortgage loan, or their respective agents may investigate the accuracy of my statements, may require me to provide additional supporting documentation and that knowingly submitting false information may violate Federal or other applicable law.

3. I authorize and give permission to the Servicer, the U.S. Department of the Treasury, and their respective agents, to assemble and use a current consumer report on all borrowers obligated on the loan, to investigate each borrower's eligibility for MHA and the accuracy of my statements and any documentation that I provide in connection with my request for assistance. I understand that these consumer reports may include, without limitation, a credit report, and be assembled and used at any point during the application process to assess each borrower's eligibility thereafter.

4. I understand that if I have intentionally defaulted on my existing mortgage, engaged in fraud or if it is determined that any of my statements or any information contained in the documentation that I provide are materially false and that I was ineligible for assistance under MHA, the Servicer, the U.S. Department of the Treasury, or their respective agents may terminate my participation in MHA, including any right to future benefits and incentives that otherwise would have been available under the program, and also may seek other remedies available at law and in equity, such as recouping any benefits or incentives previously received.

5. I certify that any property for which I am requesting assistance is a habitable residential property that is not subject to a condemnation notice.

6. I certify that I am willing to provide all requested documents and to respond to all Servicer communications in a timely manner. I understand that time is of the essence.

7. I understand that the Servicer will use the information I provide to evaluate my eligibility for available relief options and foreclosure alternatives, but the Servicer is not obligated to offer me assistance based solely on the representations in this document or other documentation submitted in connection with my request.

8. I am willing to commit to credit counseling if it is determined that my financial hardship is related to excessive debt.

9. If I am eligible for assistance under MHA, and I accept and agree to all terms of an MHA notice, plan, or agreement, I also agree that the terms of this Acknowledgment and Agreement are incorporated into such notice, plan, or agreement by reference as if set forth therein in full. My first timely payment, if required, following my servicer's determination and notification of my eligibility or prequalification for MHA assistance will serve as my acceptance of the terms set forth in the notice, plan, or agreement sent to me.

10. I understand that my Servicer will collect and record personal information that I submit in this Hardship Affidavit and during the evaluation process, including, but not limited to, my name, address, telephone number, social security number, credit score, income, payment history, government monitoring information, and information about my account balances and activity. I understand and consent to the Servicer's disclosure of my personal information and the terms of any MHA notice, plan or agreement to the U.S. Department of the Treasury and its agents, Fannie Mae and Freddie Mac in connection with their responsibilities under MHA, companies that perform support services in conjunction with MHA, any investor, insurer, guarantor, or servicer that owns, insures, guarantees, or services my first lien or subordinate lien (if applicable) mortgage loan(s) and to any HUD-certified housing counselor.

11. I consent to being contacted concerning this request for mortgage assistance at any e-mail address or cellular or mobile telephone number I have provided to the Servicer. This includes text messages and telephone calls to my cellular or mobile telephone.

The undersigned certifies under penalty of perjury that all statements in this document are true and correct.

| Borrower Signature | Social Security Number | Date of Birth | Date |

| Coborrower Signature | Social Security Number | Date of Birth | Date |

HOMEOWNER'S HOTLINE

If you have questions about this document or the Making Home Affordable Program, please call your servicer.

If you have questions about the program that your servicer cannot answer or need further counseling, you can call the Homeowner's HOPE™ Hotline at 1-888-995-HOPE (4673). The Hotline can help with questions about the program and offers free HUD-certified counseling services in English and Spanish.

888-995-HOPE
Homeowner's HOPE™ Hotline

NOTICE TO BORROWERS

Be advised that by signing this document you understand that any documents and information you submit to your servicer in connection with the Making Home Affordable Program are under penalty of perjury. Any misstatement of material fact made in the completion of these documents including but not limited to misstatement regarding your occupancy of your property, hardship circumstances, and/or income, expenses, or assets will subject you to potential criminal investigation and prosecution for the following crimes: perjury, false statements, mail fraud, and wire fraud. The information contained in these documents is subject to examination and verification. Any potential misrepresentation will be referred to the appropriate law enforcement authority for investigation and prosecution. By signing this document you certify, represent and agree that: "Under penalty of perjury, all documents and information I have provided to my Servicer in connection with the Making Home Affordable Program, including the documents and information regarding my eligibility for the program, are true and correct."

If you are aware of fraud, waste, abuse, mismanagement or misrepresentation affiliated with the Troubled Asset Relief Program, please contact the SIGTARP Hotline by calling 1-877-SIG-2009 (toll-free), 202-622-4559 (fax), or www.sigtarp.gov and provide them with your name, our name as your servicer, your property address, loan number and the reason for escalation. Mail can be sent to Hotline Office of the Special Inspector General for Troubled Asset Relief Program, 1801 L St. NW, Washington, DC 20220

Beware of Foreclosure Rescue Scams. Help is FREE!

- There is never a fee to get assistance or information about the Making Home Affordable Program from your lender or a HUD-approved housing counselor.
- Beware of any person or organization that asks you to pay a fee in exchange for housing counseling services or modification of a delinquent loan.
- Beware of anyone who says they can "save" your home if you sign or transfer over the deed to your house. Do not sign over the deed to your property to any organization or individual unless you are working directly with your mortgage company to forgive your debt.
- Never make your mortgage payments to anyone other than your mortgage company without their approval.

page 3 of 3

DODD-FRANK CERTIFICATION

HELP FOR AMERICA'S HOMEOWNERS

MAKING HOME AFFORDABLE

Dodd-Frank Certification

The following information is requested by the federal government in accordance with the Dodd-Frank Wall Street Reform and Consumer Protection Act (Pub. L. 111-203). **You are required to furnish this information.** The law provides that no person shall be eligible to begin receiving assistance from the Making Home Affordable Program, authorized under the Emergency Economic Stabilization Act of 2008 (12 U.S.C. 5201 *et seq.*), or any other mortgage assistance program authorized or funded by that Act, if such person, in connection with a mortgage or real estate transaction, has been convicted, within the last 10 years, of any one of the following: (A) felony larceny, theft, fraud, or forgery, (B) money laundering or (C) tax evasion.

I/we certify under penalty of perjury that I/we have not been convicted within the last 10 years of any one of the following in connection with a mortgage or real estate transaction:

  (a) felony larceny, theft, fraud, or forgery,
  (b) money laundering or
  (c) tax evasion.

I/we understand that the servicer, the U.S. Department of the Treasury, or their agents may investigate the accuracy of my statements by performing routine background checks, including automated searches of federal, state and county databases, to confirm that I/we have not been convicted of such crimes. I/we also understand that knowingly submitting false information may violate Federal law.

This Certificate is effective on the earlier of the date listed below or the date received by your servicer.

▶ _____   _____   _____   _____
Borrower Signature   Social Security Number   Date of Birth   Date

▶ _____   _____   _____   _____
Co-Borrower Signature   Social Security Number   Date of Birth   Date

IRS FORM 4506-T

Form **4506-T**	Request for Transcript of Tax Return	
(Rev. January 2008)	► Do not sign this form unless all applicable lines have been completed. Read the instructions on page 2.	OMB No. 1545-1872
Department of the Treasury Internal Revenue Service	► Request may be rejected if the form is incomplete, illegible, or any required line was blank at the time of signature.	

Tip: Use Form 4506-T to order a transcript or other return information free of charge. See the product list below. You can also call 1-800-829-1040 to order a transcript. If you need a copy of your return, use Form 4506, Request for Copy of Tax Return. There is a fee to get a copy of your return.

1a Name shown on tax return. If a joint return, enter the name shown first.	1b First social security number on tax return or employer identification number (see instructions)
2a If a joint return, enter spouse's name shown on tax return	2b Second social security number if joint tax return

3 Current name, address (including apt., room, or suite no.), city, state, and ZIP code

4 Previous address shown on the last return filed if different from line 3

5 If the transcript or tax information is to be mailed to a third party (such as a mortgage company), enter the third party's name, address, and telephone number. The IRS has no control over what the third party does with the tax information.

Caution: *DO NOT SIGN this form if a third party requires you to complete Form 4506-T, and lines 6 and 9 are blank.*

6 **Transcript requested.** Enter the tax form number here (1040, 1065, 1120, etc.) and check the appropriate box below. Enter only one tax form number per request. ► _____

a **Return Transcript,** which includes most of the line items of a tax return as filed with the IRS. Transcripts are only available for the following returns: Form 1040 series, Form 1065, Form 1120, Form 1120A, Form 1120H, Form 1120L, and Form 1120S. Return transcripts are available for the current year and returns processed during the prior 3 processing years. Most requests will be processed within 10 business days . . . . □

b **Account Transcript,** which contains information on the financial status of the account, such as payments made on the account, penalty assessments, and adjustments made by you or the IRS after the return was filed. Return information is limited to items such as tax liability and estimated tax payments. Account transcripts are available for most returns. Most requests will be processed within 30 calendar days . □

c **Record of Account,** which is a combination of line item information and later adjustments to the account. Available for current year and 3 prior tax years. Most requests will be processed within 30 calendar days . . . . □

7 **Verification of Nonfiling,** which is proof from the IRS that you did not file a return for the year. Most requests will be processed within 10 business days . . . . □

8 **Form W-2, Form 1099 series, Form 1098 series, or Form 5498 series transcript.** The IRS can provide a transcript that includes data from these information returns. State or local information is not included with the Form W-2 information. The IRS may be able to provide this transcript information for up to 10 years. Information for the current year is generally not available until the year after it is filed with the IRS. For example, W-2 information for 2006, filed in 2007, will not be available from the IRS until 2008. If you need W-2 information for retirement purposes, you should contact the Social Security Administration at 1-800-772-1213. Most requests will be processed within 45 days . . . . □

Caution: *If you need a copy of Form W-2 or Form 1099, you should first contact the payer. To get a copy of the Form W-2 or Form 1099 filed with your return, you must use Form 4506 and request a copy of your return, which includes all attachments.*

9 **Year or period requested.** Enter the ending date of the year or period, using the mm/dd/yyyy format. If you are requesting more than four years or periods, you must attach another Form 4506-T. For requests relating to quarterly tax returns, such as Form 941, you must enter each quarter or tax period separately.

/ /   / /   / /   / /

Signature of taxpayer(s). I declare that I am either the taxpayer whose name is shown on line 1a or 2a, or a person authorized to obtain the tax information requested. If the request applies to a joint return, either husband or wife must sign. If signed by a corporate officer, partner, guardian, tax matters partner, executor, receiver, administrator, trustee, or party other than the taxpayer, I certify that I have the authority to execute Form 4506-T on behalf of the taxpayer.

		Telephone number of taxpayer on line 1a or 2a ( )
Sign Here	► Signature (see instructions)	Date
	Title (if line 1a above is a corporation, partnership, estate, or trust)	
	► Spouse's signature	Date

For Privacy Act and Paperwork Reduction Act Notice, see page 2.   Cat. No. 37667N   Form **4506-T** (Rev. 1-2008)

General Instructions

Purpose of form. Use Form 4506-T to request tax return information. You can also designate a third party to receive the information. See line 5.

Tip. Use Form 4506, Request for Copy of Tax Return, to request copies of tax returns.

Where to file. Mail or fax Form 4506-T to the address below for the state you lived in, or the state your business was in, when that return was filed. There are two address charts: one for individual transcripts (Form 1040 series and Form W-2) and one for all other transcripts.

If you are requesting more than one transcript or other product and the chart below shows two different RAIVS teams, send your request to the team based on the address of your most recent return.

Note. You can also call 1-800-829-1040 to request a transcript or get more information.

Chart for individual transcripts (Form 1040 series and Form W-2)

If you filed an individual return and lived in:	Mail or fax to the "Internal Revenue Service" at:
District of Columbia, Maine, Maryland, Massachusetts, New Hampshire, New York, Vermont	RAIVS Team Stop 679 Andover, MA 05501 978-247-9255
Alabama, Delaware, Florida, Georgia, North Carolina, Rhode Island, South Carolina, Virginia	RAIVS Team P.O. Box 47-421 Stop 91 Doraville, GA 30362 770-455-2335
Kentucky, Louisiana, Mississippi, Tennessee, Texas, a foreign country, or A.P.O. or F.P.O. address	RAIVS Team Stop 6716 AUSC Austin, TX 73301 512-460-2272
Alaska, Arizona, California, Colorado, Hawaii, Idaho, Iowa, Kansas, Minnesota, Montana, Nebraska, Nevada, New Mexico, North Dakota, Oklahoma, Oregon, South Dakota, Utah, Washington, Wisconsin, Wyoming	RAIVS Team Stop 37106 Fresno, CA 93888 559-456-5876
Arkansas, Connecticut, Illinois, Indiana, Michigan, Missouri, New Jersey, Ohio, Pennsylvania, West Virginia	RAIVS Team Stop 6705-B41 Kansas City, MO 64999 816-292-6102

Chart for all other transcripts

If you lived in or your business was in:	Mail or fax to the "Internal Revenue Service" at:
Alabama, Alaska, Arizona, Arkansas, California, Colorado, Florida, Georgia, Hawaii, Idaho, Iowa, Kansas, Louisiana, Minnesota, Mississippi, Missouri, Montana, Nebraska, Nevada, New Mexico, North Dakota, Oklahoma, Oregon, South Dakota, Tennessee, Texas, Utah, Washington, Wyoming, a foreign country, or A.P.O. or F.P.O. address	RAIVS Team P.O. Box 9941 Mail Stop 6734 Ogden, UT 84409 801-620-6922
Connecticut, Delaware, District of Columbia, Illinois, Indiana, Kentucky, Maine, Maryland, Massachusetts, Michigan, New Hampshire, New Jersey, New York, North Carolina, Ohio, Pennsylvania, Rhode Island, South Carolina, Vermont, Virginia, West Virginia, Wisconsin	RAIVS Team P.O. Box 145500 Stop 2800 F Cincinnati, OH 45250 859-669-3592

Line 1b. Enter your employer identification number (EIN) if your request relates to a business return. Otherwise, enter the first social security number (SSN) shown on the return. For example, if you are requesting Form 1040 that includes Schedule C (Form 1040), enter your SSN.

Line 6. Enter only one tax form number per request.

Signature and date. Form 4506-T must be signed and dated by the taxpayer listed on line 1a or 2a. If you completed line 5 requesting the information be sent to a third party, the IRS must receive Form 4506-T within 60 days of the date signed by the taxpayer or it will be rejected.

Individuals. Transcripts of jointly filed tax returns may be furnished to either spouse. Only one signature is required. Sign Form 4506-T exactly as your name appeared on the original return. If you changed your name, also sign your current name.

Corporations. Generally, Form 4506-T can be signed by: (1) an officer having legal authority to bind the corporation, (2) any person designated by the board of directors or other governing body, or (3) any officer or employee on written request by any principal officer and attested to by the secretary or other officer.

Partnerships. Generally, Form 4506-T can be signed by any person who was a member of the partnership during any part of the tax period requested on line 9.

All others. See Internal Revenue Code section 6103(e) if the taxpayer has died, is insolvent, is a dissolved corporation, or if a trustee, guardian, executor, receiver, or administrator is acting for the taxpayer.

Documentation. For entities other than individuals, you must attach the authorization document. For example, this could be the letter from the principal officer authorizing an employee of the corporation or the Letters Testamentary authorizing an individual to act for an estate.

Privacy Act and Paperwork Reduction Act Notice. We ask for the information on this form to establish your right to gain access to the requested tax information under the Internal Revenue Code. We need this information to properly identify the tax information and respond to your request. Sections 6103 and 6109 require you to provide this information, including your SSN or EIN. If you do not provide this information, we may not be able to process your request. Providing false or fraudulent information may subject you to penalties.

Routine uses of this information include giving it to the Department of Justice for civil and criminal litigation, and cities, states, and the District of Columbia for use in administering their tax laws. We may also disclose this information to other countries under a tax treaty, to federal and state agencies to enforce federal nontax criminal laws, or to federal law enforcement and intelligence agencies to combat terrorism.

You are not required to provide the information requested on a form that is subject to the Paperwork Reduction Act unless the form displays a valid OMB control number. Books or records relating to a form or its instructions must be retained as long as their contents may become material in the administration of any Internal Revenue law. Generally, tax returns and return information are confidential, as required by section 6103.

The time needed to complete and file Form 4506-T will vary depending on individual circumstances. The estimated average time is: **Learning about the law or the form,** 10 min.; **Preparing the form,** 12 min.; and **Copying, assembling, and sending the form to the IRS,** 20 min.

If you have comments concerning the accuracy of these time estimates or suggestions for making Form 4506-T simpler, we would be happy to hear from you. You can write to the Internal Revenue Service, Tax Products Coordinating Committee, SE:W:CAR:MP:T:T:SP, 1111 Constitution Ave. NW, IR-6526, Washington, DC 20224. Do not send the form to this address. Instead, see *Where to file* on this page.

Form 4506T-EZ

(Rev. January 2012)

Department of the Treasury
Internal Revenue Service

Short Form Request for Individual Tax Return Transcript

OMB No. 1545-2154

▶ Request may not be processed if the form is incomplete or illegible.

Tip. Use Form 4506T-EZ to order a 1040 series tax return transcript free of charge, or you can quickly request transcripts by using our automated self-help service tools. Please visit us at IRS.gov and click on "Order a Transcript" or call 1-800-908-9946.

1a Name shown on tax return. If a joint return, enter the name shown first.	1b First social security number or individual taxpayer identification number on tax return
2a If a joint return, enter spouse's name shown on tax return.	2b Second social security number or individual taxpayer identification number if joint tax return

3 Current name, address (including apt., room, or suite no.), city, state, and ZIP code (see instructions)

4 Previous address shown on the last return filed if different from line 3 (see instructions)

5 If the transcript is to be mailed to a third party (such as a mortgage company), enter the third party's name, address, and telephone number. The IRS has no control over what the third party does with the tax information.

Third party name	Telephone number

Address (including apt., room, or suite no.), city, state, and ZIP code

Caution. If the tax transcript is being mailed to a third party, ensure that you have filled in line 6 before signing. Sign and date the form once you have filled in this line. Completing this step helps to protect your privacy. Once the IRS discloses your IRS transcript to the third party listed on line 5, the IRS has no control over what the third party does with the information. If you would like to limit the third party's authority to disclose your transcript information, you can specify this limitation in your written agreement with the third party.

6 **Year(s) requested.** Enter the year(s) of the return transcript you are requesting (for example, "2008"). Most requests will be processed within 10 business days.

_____ _____ _____ _____

☐ Check this box if you have notified the IRS or the IRS has notified you that one of the years for which you are requesting a transcript involved **identity theft** on your federal tax return.

Note. If the IRS is unable to locate a return that matches the taxpayer identity information provided above, or if IRS records indicate that the return has not been filed, the IRS may notify you or the third party that it was unable to locate a return, or that a return was not filed, whichever is applicable.

Caution. Do not sign this form unless all applicable lines have been completed.

Signature of taxpayer(s). I declare that I am the taxpayer whose name is shown on either line 1a or 2a. If the request applies to a joint return, **either** husband or wife must sign. **Note.** For transcripts being sent to a third party, this form must be received within 120 days of the signature date.

		Phone number of taxpayer on line 1a or 2a

Sign Here ▶

Signature (see instructions)	Date

▶

Spouse's signature	Date

For Privacy Act and Paperwork Reduction Act Notice, see page 2.   Cat. No. 54185S   Form **4506T-EZ** (Rev. 1-2012)

Section references are to the Internal Revenue Code unless otherwise noted.

What's New

The IRS has created a page on IRS.gov for information about Form 4506T-EZ at http://www.irs.gov/form4506. Information about any recent developments affecting Form 4506T-EZ (such as legislation enacted after we released it) will be posted on that page.

Caution. Do not sign this form unless all applicable lines have been completed.

Purpose of form. Individuals can use Form 4506T-EZ to request a tax return transcript for the current and the prior three years that includes most lines of the original tax return. The tax return transcript will not show payments, penalty assessments, or adjustments made to the originally filed return. You can also designate (on line 5) a third party (such as a mortgage company) to receive a transcript. Form 4506T-EZ cannot be used by taxpayers who file Form 1040 based on a tax year beginning in one calendar year and ending in the following year (fiscal tax year). Taxpayers using a fiscal tax year must file Form 4506-T, Request for Transcript of Tax Return, to request a return transcript.

Use Form 4506-T to request tax return transcripts, tax account information, W-2 information, 1099 information, verification of non-filing, and record of account.

Automated transcript request. You can quickly request transcripts by using our automated self-help service tools. Please visit us at IRS.gov and click on "Order a Transcript" or call 1-800-908-9946.

Where to file. Mail or fax Form 4506T-EZ to the address below for the state you lived in when the return was filed.

If you are requesting more than one transcript or other product and the chart below shows two different addresses, send your request to the address based on the address of your most recent return.

If you filed an individual return and lived in:	Mail or fax to the "Internal Revenue Service" at:
Alabama, Kentucky, Louisiana, Mississippi, Tennessee, Texas, a foreign country, American Samoa, Puerto Rico, Guam, the Commonwealth of the Northern Mariana Islands, the U.S. Virgin Islands, or A.P.O. or F.P.O. address	RAIVS Team Stop 6716 AUSC Austin, TX 73301 512-460-2272
Alaska, Arizona, Arkansas, California, Colorado, Hawaii, Idaho, Illinois, Indiana, Iowa, Kansas, Michigan, Minnesota, Montana, Nebraska, Nevada, New Mexico, North Dakota, Oklahoma, Oregon, South Dakota, Utah, Washington, Wisconsin, Wyoming	RAIVS Team Stop 37106 Fresno, CA 93888 559-456-5876
Connecticut, Delaware, District of Columbia, Florida, Georgia, Maine, Maryland, Massachusetts, Missouri, New Hampshire, New Jersey, New York, North Carolina, Ohio, Pennsylvania, Rhode Island, South Carolina, Vermont, Virginia, West Virginia	RAIVS Team Stop 6705 P-6 Kansas City, MO 64999 816-292-6102

Line 1b. Enter your employer identification number (EIN) if your request relates to a business return. Otherwise, enter the first social security number (SSN) or your individual taxpayer identification number (ITIN) shown on the return. For example, if you are requesting Form 1040 that includes Schedule C (Form 1040), enter your SSN.

Line 3. Enter your current address. If you use a P.O. box, include it on this line.

Line 4. Enter the address shown on the last return filed if different from the address entered on line 3.

Note. If the address on lines 3 and 4 are different and you have not changed your address with the IRS, file Form 8822, Change of Address.

Signature and date. Form 4506T-EZ must be signed and dated by the taxpayer listed on line 1a or 2a. If you completed line 5 requesting the information be sent to a third party, the IRS must receive Form 4506T-EZ within 120 days of the date signed by the taxpayer or it will be rejected. Ensure that all applicable lines are completed before signing.

Transcripts of jointly filed tax returns may be furnished to either spouse. Only one signature is required. Sign Form 4506T-EZ exactly as your name appeared on the original return. If you changed your name, also sign your current name.

Privacy Act and Paperwork Reduction Act Notice. We ask for the information on this form to establish your right to gain access to the requested tax information under the Internal Revenue Code. We need this information to properly identify the tax information and respond to your request. If you request a transcript, sections 6103 and 6109 require you to provide this information, including your SSN. If you do not provide this information, we may not be able to process your request. Providing false or fraudulent information may subject you to penalties.

Routine uses of this information include giving it to the Department of Justice for civil and criminal litigation, and cities, states, the District of Columbia, and U.S. commonwealths and possessions for use in administering their tax laws. We may also disclose this information to other countries under a tax treaty, to federal and state agencies to enforce federal nontax criminal laws, or to federal law enforcement and intelligence agencies to combat terrorism.

You are not required to provide the information requested on a form that is subject to the Paperwork Reduction Act unless the form displays a valid OMB control number. Books or records relating to a form or its instructions must be retained as long as their contents may become material in the administration of any Internal Revenue law. Generally, tax returns and return information are confidential, as required by section 6103.

The time needed to complete and file Form 4506T-EZ will vary depending on individual circumstances. The estimated average time is: **Learning about the law or the form,** 9 min.; **Preparing the form,** 18 min.; and **Copying, assembling, and sending the form to the IRS,** 20 min.

If you have comments concerning the accuracy of these time estimates or suggestions for making Form 4506T-EZ simpler, we would be happy to hear from you. You can write to:

Internal Revenue Service
Tax Products Coordinating Committee
SE:W:CAR:MP:T:M:S
1111 Constitution Ave. NW, IR-6526
Washington, DC 20224

Do not send the form to this address. Instead, see Where to file on this page.

REQUEST FOR APPROVAL OF SHORT SALE

HELP FOR AMERICA'S HOMEOWNERS.

MAKING HOME AFFORDABLE

[Name of Servicer] [Address of Servicer]	[Name of Borrower] [Name of Co-Borrower] [Address of Borrower]
[Loan #] [Servicer FAX] [Servicer Email]	[Borrower Phone] [Borrower Email]

[Date]

RE: Request for Approval of Short Sale Pursuant to Agreement Dated [Date of SSA]

This is a Request for Approval of the Short Sale Pursuant to Agreement Dated [Date of SSA] between the above referenced Servicer ("Servicer") and the borrower and co-borrower ("Borrower" or "you"). By submitting this Request, you certify under penalty of perjury that:

1) the sale of the property is an "arm's length" transaction, between parties who are unrelated and unaffiliated by family, marriage, or commercial enterprise;
2) there are no agreements or understandings between you and the Buyer that you will remain in the property as a tenant or later obtain title or ownership of the property;
3) neither you nor the Buyer will receive any funds or commissions from the sale of the property;
4) there are no agreements or offers relating to the sale or subsequent sale of the property that have not been disclosed to the Servicer; and
5) any occupant (whether (i) you or (ii) a tenant (or your legal dependent, parent or grandparent who is living in the property rent free) ("Tenant")) for whom you are requesting relocation assistance occupies the property as his or her principal residence and is required to vacate the property as a condition of the sale.

Please complete, sign and return the Terms of Sale on the following page.

Program Terms And Conditions

MAKING HOME AFFORDABLE

Terms of Sale [All blanks to be completed by Borrower]:

1. Contract Sales Price	$		6. Closing Date:	
2. Less Total Allowable Closing Costs	$		7. Approved Buyer(s):	
a. Commissions	$			
b. Settlement Escrow/Attorney Fees	$			
c. Seller's Title and Escrow Fees	$		8. Settlement Agent:	
d. Subordinate Lien Payoff	$			
e. Transfer taxes/stamps/recording fees	$			
f. Real Property Taxes	$		9. Settlement Agent's Address:	
g. Termite Inspection/Repair	$			
h. Relocation Assistance	$			
i. Other (attach explanation)	$			
3. Net Proceeds to Servicer	$			
4. Earnest Money Deposit	$		10. Settlement Agent's Office Phone:	
5. Down Payment	$		11. Settlement Agent's Office Fax:	

As required by the Short Sale Agreement, copies of the following documents are attached:

❏ Sales contract and all addenda

❏ Buyer's documentation of funds or Buyer's pre-approval or commitment letter on letterhead from lender

❏ Evidence that the property is occupied as a principal residence by you or a Tenant who will be required to vacate as a condition of the sale. [Only required if the borrower is requesting Relocation Assistance.]

❏ Completed Hardship Affidavit and Dodd-Frank Certification(s) signed by the borrower if not previously provided.

❏ Completed Dodd-Frank Certification(s) signed by any Tenant that will receive Relocation Assistance. [Only required if the borrower is requesting Relocation Assistance for a Tenant.]

If not attached, the servicer must have these documents no later than [insert date 14 calendar days from date of this request] or we will not be able to respond to this request. Please send us any missing documents at the following address: [insert servicer address].

The Borrower represents that the information provided in this Request is true and accurate and authorizes the Servicer to disclose to the U.S. Department of the Treasury or other government agency, Fannie Mae and/or Freddie Mac any information provided in connection with the Making Home Affordable program.

Borrower Signature	Date	Co- Borrower Signature	Date
Printed Name		Printed Name	

If you would like to speak with a counselor about this program, call the Homeowners HOPE™ Hotline 1-888-995-HOPE (4673). The Homeowner's HOPE™ Hotline offers free HUD-certified counseling services and is available 24/7 in English and Spanish. Other languages are available by appointment.

If you have questions, please contact us directly between the hours of [insert hours] at [insert toll free number.]

To be Completed by Your Servicer

Approval of Short Sale - The Servicer consents to this Request for Approval of Short Sale and agrees to accept all net proceeds from the settlement as full and final satisfaction of the first mortgage indebtedness on the referenced property. This agreement is subject to the following:

A. **Terms** – The sale and closing comply with all terms and conditions of the Short Sale Agreement between the Servicer and the Borrower as well as all terms and representations provided herein by the Borrower.

B. **Changes** – Any change to the terms and representations contained in this Request for Approval of Short Sale or the attached sales contract between you and the buyer must be approved by the Servicer in writing. The Servicer is under no obligation to approve such changes.

C. **Subordinate Liens** – Prior to releasing any funds to holders of subordinate liens/mortgages, the closing agent must obtain a written commitment from the subordinate lien holder that it will release Borrower from all claims and liability relating to the subordinate lien in exchange for receiving the agreed upon payoff amount.

D. **HUD-1** – A HUD-1 Settlement Statement, which will be signed by you and the buyer at closing, must be provided to the Servicer not later than one business day before the date indicated in Line 4, *Closing Date*.

E. **Bankruptcy** – If you are currently in bankruptcy or you file bankruptcy prior to closing, you must obtain any required consent or approval of the Bankruptcy Court.

F. **Tax Consequences** – A short payoff of the mortgage may have tax consequences. You are advised to contact a tax professional to determine the extent of tax liability, if any.

G. **Credit Bureau Reporting** – We will follow standard industry practice and report to the major credit reporting agencies that your mortgage was settled for less than the full payment. We have no control over or responsibility for the impact of this report on your credit score. To learn more about the potential impact of a short sale on your credit you may want to go to http://www.ftc.gov/bcp/edu/pubs/consumer/credit/cre24.shtm.

H. **Payment Instructions** – Payoff funds and a final HUD-1 Settlement Statement must be received by the Servicer within 48 hours of closing in accordance with the attached wiring instructions. *[include instructions]*

I. **Closing Instructions** – *[include proprietary closing instructions, if any including instructions for delivery of a Dodd-Frank Certification executed by any occupant that will receive relocation assistance if not already received by the servicer.]*

If you have questions, please contact us directly between the hours of [insert hours] at [insert toll free number.]

_____   _____
Signature of Servicer Representative   Title

_____   _____
Printed Name of Servicer Representative   Date

Servicer Use Only

MAKING HOME AFFORDABLE

To be Completed by Your Servicer

Disapproval of Short Sale - The Servicer disapproves this Request for Approval of Short Sale, for the following reasons (check all applicable reasons):

☐	You did not comply with all terms and conditions of the Short Sale Agreement between Servicer and Borrower dated _____/_____/_____ as it relates to section/s: _____ _____

☐	The Request for Approval of Short Sale was not complete and/or fully executed.
	   ☐ Failure to provide executed sales contract or addenda
	   ☐ Failure to provide buyer's documentation of funds to close or buyer's pre-approval or commitment letter on letterhead from lender

☐	The net proceeds available to pay off the first mortgage loan are insufficient, due to:
	   ☐ Contract sales price is below list price stated in Short Sale Agreement
	   ☐ Net proceeds amount is less than acceptable net proceeds stated in Short Sale Agreement
	   ☐ Excessive financial concessions
	   ☐ Excessive commissions
	   ☐ Excessive closing costs
	   ☐ Excessive payments to subordinate liens/mortgages OR release of subordinate liens did not occur

☐	The mortgage insurer did not approve the short sale.
☐	Other:

If you have questions, please contact us directly between the hours of [insert hours] at [insert toll free number.]

_____   _____
Signature of Servicer Representative   Title

_____   _____
Printed Name of Servicer Representative   Date

APPENDIX 6

ALTERNATIVE RASS

HELP FOR AMERICA'S HOMEOWNERS.

MAKING HOME AFFORDABLE

[Name of Servicer]   [Name of Borrower]
[Address of Servicer]   [Name of Co-Borrower]
                                                      [Address of Borrower]

[Loan #]
[Servicer FAX]   [Borrower Phone]
[Servicer Email]   [Borrower Email]

[Date]

RE: Request for Approval of Short Sale

You have taken an important step toward selling your residential property and avoiding foreclosure by participating in the federal government's **Home Affordable Foreclosure Alternatives** (HAFA) Program. This letter is a Request for Approval of a Short Sale and contains important information.

Read the following pages carefully and complete, sign and return the Terms and Conditions.

If you have not previously contacted us regarding eligibility for a loan modification, you should consider this alternative. Under the Home Affordable Modification Program (HAMP), you may qualify for a modification with affordable and sustainable monthly payments that would allow you to keep your property. Please contact us by *[insert date 14 calendar days from date of this request]* if you wish to be considered for a loan modification.

If you have questions, please contact us directly between the hours of [insert hours] at [insert toll free number.]

Sincerely,

[Servicer Name]

1

Program Terms And Conditions	

The borrower and co-borrower, if applicable ("Borrower" or "you"), of the above loan contacted the Servicer ("Servicer" or "we") because your mortgage payments are no longer affordable and you would like to avoid foreclosure. After listing your residential property for sale, an offer was received. However, the sale may not be sufficient to pay off the loan. This is a Request for Approval of a Short Sale ("Request") of the subject property, the net sale proceeds from which we agree to accept as the payoff of the mortgage loan even though the proceeds are expected to be less than the full amount due.

Short Sale Program—Terms and Conditions of the Request are as follows:

1. **Allowable Costs that May be Deducted from Gross Sale Proceeds**
   a. **Closing Costs.** The closing costs paid by you or on your behalf as seller must be reasonable and customary for the market. [*Choose one and delete unnecessary text.*] [Acceptable closing costs, including the commission, which may be deducted from the gross sale proceeds may not exceed $_____.] OR [Acceptable closing costs, including the commission, which may be deducted from the gross sale proceeds may not exceed ____% of the list price.] OR [Closing costs which may be deducted from the gross sale proceeds are limited to title search and escrow expenses usually paid by the seller; reasonable settlement escrow/attorney's fees; transfer taxes and recording fees usually paid by the seller; termite inspection and treatment as required by law or custom; pro-rated real property taxes; and, negotiated real estate commissions not to exceed six percent (6%) of the contract sales price [add other closing costs that may be included].]

   b. **Subordinate Liens.** We will allow a total of up to (i) [*insert the lesser of $8,500 or maximum amount allowable by investor*] to pay subordinate mortgage lien holders to release their mortgage liens and (ii) [*choose one as applicable*] [$_____] OR [_____% of the gross sale proceeds] [*insert amount or percentage, as applicable and as determined by servicer*] to pay subordinate non-mortgage lien holders to release their non-mortgage liens, in each case to be deducted from gross sale proceeds. We require each subordinate lien holder to release you from personal liability for the loans in order for the sale to qualify for this program, but we do not take any responsibility for ensuring that the lien holders do not seek to enforce personal liability against you. Therefore, we recommend that you take steps to satisfy yourself that the subordinate lien holders release you from personal liability.

   c. **Real Estate Commissions.** We will allow to be paid from sale proceeds, real estate commissions as stated in the listing agreement between you and your broker, not to exceed six percent (6%) of the contract sales price, to be paid to the listing and selling brokers involved in the transaction. Neither you nor the buyer may receive a commission. Any commission that would otherwise be paid to you or the buyer must be reduced from the commission due on sale. [*insert if applicable*: Please note: We have retained a vendor to assist your listing broker with the sale. The vendor and your listing broker will work together on your behalf to facilitate the sale process. Vendor fees or charges will not be charged to you and will not be deducted from the real estate commission. Additionally, any outsourcing firm or third party retained as an agent for us may not charge (either directly or indirectly) any outsourcing fee, short sale negotiation fee, or similar fee in connection with the short sale.]

   d. [*Section may be omitted if the property is vacant*]: Occupant Relocation Assistance. If the closing of the short sale occurs in accordance with this Agreement and the property is occupied as a principal residence by (i) you or (ii) a tenant (or your legal dependent, parent or grandparent who is living in the property rent free)("Tenant") who will be required to vacate as a condition of the sale, you or the Tenant may be entitled to an incentive payment of $3,000 to assist with relocation expenses. To request relocation assistance for yourself or your Tenant, you must provide (i)_evidence that the property is your/their principal residence, which in the case of a Tenant may include information concerning the tenant, a copy of the lease agreement or other evidence of occupancy; and (ii) a certification signed by each occupant that will receive relocation assistance, attesting to the occupant's compliance with Section 1481 of the Dodd-Frank Wall Street Reform and Consumer Protection Act (Pub. L. 111-203) (the Dodd-Frank Certification). Upon request we will provide you with a Dodd-Frank Certification form(s). If you fail to deliver the Dodd-Frank Certification at least ___ days prior to the closing of the sale of the property, the

2

incentive payment will not be paid. Upon your compliance with the terms of this Agreement, we will instruct the settlement agent to pay the occupant from the sale proceeds at the same time that all other payments, including the payoff of our first mortgage, are disbursed by the settlement agent. Only one payment per household is provided for the relocation assistance, regardless of the number of occupants.]

2. **Property Maintenance and Expenses.** You are responsible for all property maintenance and expenses of your property until the closing of an approved short sale, including utilities, assessments, association dues, and costs for interior and exterior maintenance. Additionally, you must report any and all property damage to us and file a hazard insurance claim for covered damage. Unless insurance proceeds are used to pay for repairs or personal property losses, we may require that they be applied to reduce the mortgage debt.

3. *[Insert only if applicable:]* **Partial Mortgage Payments.** Beginning on _____ 1, 20___, you will be required to make partial mortgage payments of $_____ by the first day of each month during the term of the Request and pending transfer of property ownership. You are legally obligated to make the full amount of your current monthly mortgage payments. However, we will accept this reduced partial payment until the property is sold or this Agreement expires. The partial mortgage payments do not constitute a modification of your mortgage.

4. **Parties to the Sale.** The Sales Contract must include the following clauses: "Seller and Buyer each represent that the sale is an "arm's length" transaction and the Seller and Buyer are unrelated to each other by family, marriage or commercial enterprise." "The Buyer agrees not to sell the property within 90 days of closing of this sale."

5. **Foreclosure Sale Suspension.** We may initiate or continue the foreclosure process as permitted by the mortgage documents; however, we will suspend any foreclosure sale date until the expiration date of this Request or the date of closing of an approved short sale, whichever is later, provided that you abide by its terms and conditions.

6. **Satisfaction and Release of Liability.** If all of the terms and conditions of this Request are met, upon sale and settlement of the property, we will prepare and send to the settlement agent for recording, a lien release in full satisfaction of the mortgage, foregoing all rights to pursue a deficiency judgment.

7. *[Insert only if applicable.]* **Mortgage Insurer or Guarantor Approval.** The terms and conditions of the purchase contract are subject to the written approval of the mortgage insurer or guarantor.

8. **Termination of This Request.** Unless otherwise agreed by the parties, this Request will terminate on *[insert date]* if the sale does not close. This Request may be terminated earlier if:

   a. You fail to provide all the required documents listed herein

   b. Your financial situation improves significantly, you qualify for a modification, you bring the account current or you pay off the mortgage in full.

   c. You or your broker fails to act in good faith in closing on the sale of the property or otherwise fails to abide by the terms of this Request.

   d. A significant change occurs to the property condition or value.

   e. There is evidence of fraud or misrepresentation.

   f. You file for bankruptcy and the Bankruptcy Court declines to approve the Request.

   g. Litigation is initiated or threatened that could affect title to the property or interfere with a valid conveyance.

   h. *[Insert only if applicable:]* You do not make the payments required under this Request.

9. **Settlement of a Debt.** The proposed transaction represents the Servicer's attempt to reach a settlement of the delinquent mortgage. You are choosing to enter into this transaction even though there is no guarantee that the transaction will be successful. In the event this transaction is unsuccessful, the Servicer may exercise all remedies under the mortgage, including foreclosure.

3

Program Terms And Conditions

MAKING HOME AFFORDABLE

Terms of Sale [All blanks to be completed by Borrower]:

1.	Contract Sales Price	$		6.	Closing Date:
2.	Less Total Allowable Closing Costs	$		7.	Approved Buyer(s):
	a. Commissions	$			
	b. Settlement Escrow/Attorney Fees	$			
	c. Seller's Title and Escrow Fees	$		8.	Settlement Agent:
	d. Subordinate Lien Payoff	$			
	e. Transfer taxes/stamps/recording fees	$			
	f. Real Property Taxes	$		9.	Settlement Agent's Address:
	g. Termite Inspection/Repair	$			
	h. Relocation Assistance	$			
	i. Other (attach explanation)	$			
3.	Net Proceeds to Servicer	$			
4.	Earnest Money Deposit	$		10.	Settlement Agent's Office Phone:
5.	Down Payment	$		11.	Settlement Agent's Office Fax:

As required by the Short Sale Program, copies of the following documents are attached:

❑ Signed Request;

❑ Copy of a signed listing agreement with a real estate broker, if applicable;

❑ Executed copy of the sales contract and all addenda;

❑ Buyer's documentation of funds or Buyer's pre-approval or commitment letter on letterhead from a lender;

❑ Information about other liens secured by the subject property such as home-equity loans;

❑ Evidence that the property is occupied as a principal residence by you or a Tenant who will be required to vacate as a condition of the sale. [Only required if the borrower is requesting Relocation Assistance.]

❑ Completed Hardship Affidavit and Dodd-Frank Certification(s) signed by the borrower if not previously provided.

❑ Completed Dodd-Frank Certification(s) signed by any Tenant that will receive Relocation Assistance. [Only required if the borrower is requesting Relocation Assistance for the Tenant.]

If not attached, the servicer must have these documents no later than [insert date 14 calendar days from date of this request] or we will not be able to respond to this request. Please send us any missing documents at the following address: [insert servicer address].

Under penalty of perjury, you certify that:

1. the sale of the property is an "arm's-length" transaction, between parties who are unrelated and unaffiliated by family, marriage, or commercial enterprise;

2. there are no agreements or understandings between you and the Buyer that you will remain in the property as a tenant or later obtain title or ownership of the property;

3. neither you nor the Buyer will receive any funds or commissions from the sale of the property;

4. there are no agreements or offers relating to the sale or subsequent sale of the property that have not been disclosed to the Servicer; and

5. any occupant (whether you or your Tenant) for whom you are requesting relocation assistance occupies the property as his or her principal residence and is required to vacate the property as a condition of the sale.

4

Program Terms And Conditions

MAKING HOME AFFORDABLE

By signing below, I/we agree to all the stated terms and conditions of the Request, and I/we represent that the information provided in this Request is true and accurate and authorize the Servicer to disclose to the U.S. Department of the Treasury or other government agency, Fannie Mae and/or Freddie Mac any information provided in connection with the Making Home Affordable program.

Borrower Signature   Date   Co- Borrower Signature   Date

_____ _____
Printed Name   Printed Name

If you would like to speak with a counselor about this program, call the Homeowner's HOPE™ Hotline 1-888-995-HOPE (4673). The Homeowner's HOPE™ Hotline offers free HUD-certified counseling services and is available 24/7 in English and Spanish. Other languages are available by appointment.

If you have questions, please contact us directly between the hours of [insert hours] at [insert toll free number.]

NOTICE TO BORROWER

Be advised that by signing this document you understand that any documents and information you submit to your servicer in connection with the Making Home Affordable Program are under penalty of perjury. Any misstatement of material fact made in the completion of these documents including but not limited to misstatement regarding your occupancy in your home, hardship circumstances, and/or income, expenses, or assets will subject you to potential criminal investigation and prosecution for the following crimes: perjury, false statements, mail fraud, and wire fraud. The information contained in these documents is subject to examination and verification. Any potential misrepresentation will be referred to the appropriate law enforcement authority for investigation and prosecution. By signing this document you certify, represent and agree that:" Under penalty of perjury, all documents and information I have provided to lender in connection with the Making Home Affordable Program, including the documents and information regarding my eligibility for the program, are true and correct."

If you are aware of fraud, waste, abuse, mismanagement or misrepresentations affiliated with the Troubled Asset Relief Program, please contact the SIGTARP Hotline by calling 1-877-SIG-2009 (toll-free), 202-622-4559 (fax), or www.sigtarp.gov. Mail can be sent Hotline Office of the Special Inspector General for Troubled Asset Relief Program, 1801 L St. NW, Washington, DC 20220.

5

Servicer Use Only

MAKING HOME AFFORDABLE

To be Completed by Your Servicer

Approval of Short Sale - The Servicer consents to this Request for Approval of Short Sale and agrees to accept all net proceeds from the settlement as full and final satisfaction of the first mortgage indebtedness on the referenced property. This approval is subject to the following:

A. **Terms** – The sale and closing comply with all terms and conditions of the Request as well as all terms and representations provided herein by the Borrower.

B. **Changes** – Any change to the terms and representations contained in the Request or the attached sales contract between you and the buyer must be approved by the Servicer in writing. The Servicer is under no obligation to approve such changes.

C. **Subordinate Liens** – Prior to releasing any funds to holders of subordinate liens/mortgages, the closing agent must obtain a written commitment from the subordinate lien holder that it will release Borrower from all claims and liability relating to the subordinate lien in exchange for receiving the agreed upon payoff amount.

D. **HUD-1** – A HUD-1 Settlement Statement, which will be signed by you and the buyer at closing, must be provided to the Servicer not later than one business day before the date indicated in Line 4, *Closing Date*.

E. **Bankruptcy** – If you are currently in bankruptcy or you file bankruptcy prior to closing, you must obtain any required consent or approval of the Bankruptcy Court.

F. **Tax Consequences** – A short payoff of the mortgage may have tax consequences. You are advised to contact a tax professional to determine the extent of tax liability, if any.

G. **Credit Bureau Reporting** – We will follow standard industry practice and report to the major credit reporting agencies that your mortgage was settled for less than the full payment. We have no control over or responsibility for the impact of this report on your credit score. To learn more about the potential impact of a short sale on your credit you may want to go to http://www.ftc.gov/bcp/edu/pubs/consumer/credit/cre24.shtm.

H. **Payment Instructions** – Payoff funds and a final HUD-1 Settlement Statement must be received by the Servicer within 48 hours of closing in accordance with the attached wiring instructions. [*Include instructions*]

A. **Closing Instructions** – [*Include proprietary closing instructions, if any including instructions for delivery of a Dodd-Frank Certification executed by any occupant that will receive relocation assistance if not already received by servicer.*]

If you have questions, please contact us directly between the hours of [insert hours] at [insert toll free number.]

Signature of Servicer Representative	Title
Printed Name of Servicer Representative	Date

6

MAKING HOME AFFORDABLE

To be Completed by your Servicer

Disapproval of Short Sale - The Servicer disapproves this Request for Approval of Short Sale, for the following reasons (check all applicable reasons):

☐	You did not comply with all terms and conditions of the Request for Approval of Short Sale as it relates to section/s: _____

☐	The Request for Approval of Short Sale was not complete and/or fully executed.
	  ☐ Failure to provide executed sales contract or addenda
	  ☐ Failure to provide buyer's documentation of funds to close or buyer's pre-approval or commitment letter on letterhead from lender

☐	The net proceeds available to pay off the first mortgage loan are insufficient, due to:
	  ☐ Contract sales price is below list price stated in Short Sale Agreement
	  ☐ Net proceeds amount is less than acceptable net proceeds stated in Short Sale Agreement
	  ☐ Excessive financial concessions
	  ☐ Excessive commissions
	  ☐ Excessive closing costs
	  ☐ Excessive payments to subordinate liens/mortgages OR release of subordinate liens did not occur

☐	The mortgage insurer, investor or guarantor of the loan did not approve the short sale.
☐	Other:

If you have questions, please contact us directly between the hours of [insert hours] at [insert toll free number.]

_____	_____
Signature of Servicer Representative	Title
_____	_____
Printed Name of Servicer Representative	Date

7

Response Times for Borrowers and Lenders

HAFA Short Sale

Who	Days	Submit Offer	Acknowledge	Respond	Deliver SSA	Return SSA	Market Property	Approve or Deny	Close
		SCREENING			EVALUATION		MARKETING	CLOSING	
SERVICER Calendar		30			45				45+
SERVICER Business				10				10	
OWNER Calendar			14			14	120+		45+
OWNER Business							3		

HAFA Alternative Short Sale

Who	Days	Submit	Acknowledge	Notify	Respond	Approve or Deny	Close
		OFFER		HAMP		CLOSING	
SERVICER Calendar				?		45	45+
SERVICER Business			10				
OWNER Calendar		0			14		45+
OWNER Business							

THIRD PARTY AUTHORIZATION

HELP FOR AMERICA'S HOMEOWNERS.

MAKING HOME AFFORDABLE

Third-Party Authorization Form

_____   _____
Mortgage Lender/Servicer Name ("Servicer")   [Account][Loan] Number

The undersigned Borrower and Co-Borrower (if any) (individually and collectively, "Borrower" or "I"), authorize the above Servicer and the following third parties

_____   _____
[Counseling Agency]   [Agency Contact Name and Phone Number]

_____   _____
[State HFA Entity]   [State HFA Contact Name and Phone Number]

_____   _____
[Other Third Party]   [Third Party Contact Name and Phone Number]

_____
[Relationship of Other Third Party to Borrower and Co-Borrower]

(individually and collectively, "Third Party") to obtain, share, release, discuss, and otherwise provide to and with each other public and non-public personal information contained in or related to the mortgage loan of the Borrower. This information may include (but is not limited to) the name, address, telephone number, social security number, credit score, credit report, income, government monitoring information, loss mitigation application status, account balances, program eligibility, and payment activity of the Borrower. I also understand and consent to the disclosure of my personal information and the terms of any agreements under the Making Home Affordable or Hardest Hit Fund Programs by Servicer or State HFA to the U.S. Department of the Treasury or their agents in connection with their responsibilities under the Emergency Economic Stabilization Act.

The Servicer will take reasonable steps to verify the identity of a Third Party, but has no responsibility or liability to verify the identity of such Third Party. The Servicer also has no responsibility or liability for what a Third Party does with such information.

> **Before signing this Third-Party Authorization, beware of foreclosure rescue scams!**
>
> - It is expected that a HUD-approved housing counselor, HFA representative or other authorized third party will work directly with your lender/mortgage servicer.
> - Please visit http://makinghomeaffordable.gov/counselor.html to verify you are working with a HUD-approved housing counseling agency.
> - Beware of anyone who asks you to pay a fee in exchange for a counseling service or modification of a delinquent loan.

This Third-Party Authorization is valid when signed by all borrowers and co-borrowers named on the mortgage and until the Servicer receives a written revocation signed by any borrower or co-borrower.

I UNDERSTAND AND AGREE WITH THE TERMS OF THIS THIRD-PARTY AUTHORIZATION:

Borrower   Co-Borrower

_____   _____
Printed Name   Printed Name

_____ ⟨ SIGN   _____ ⟨ SI
Signature   Signature

_____   _____
Date   Date

NON-OWNER OCCUPANT (TENANT) CERTIFICATION

Making Home Affordable Program
Non-Owner Occupant Certification

MAKING HOME AFFORDABLE.gov

You are the occupant of a property that is being sold or transferred in conjunction with the U.S. Department of the Treasury's Home Affordable Foreclosure Alternative (HAFA) Program. Because you will be required to vacate the property as a condition of the sale or transfer, you may be eligible to receive $3,000 in relocation assistance. If you wish to be considered for this assistance, you must complete and sign this form and return it to the owner of the property (Owner).

OCCUPANT INFORMATION

OCCUPANT'S NAME | CO-OCCUPANT'S NAME

PROPERTY ADDRESS (Include city, state and zip)

I certify that I currently occupy the property described above (the Property) as a principal residence and, to the best of my knowledge, I am required to vacate the Property as a condition of the pending sale or transfer.

DODD-FRANK CERTIFICATION

The following information is requested by the federal government in accordance with the Dodd-Frank Wall Street Reform and Consumer Protection Act (Pub. L. 111-203). You are required to furnish this information. The law provides that no person shall be eligible to begin receiving assistance from the Making Home Affordable Program (MHA), authorized under the Emergency Economic Stabilization Act of 2008 (12 U.S.C. 5201 et seq.), or any other mortgage assistance program authorized or funded by that Act, if such person, in connection with a mortgage or real estate transaction, has been convicted, within the last 10 years, of any one of the following: (A) felony larceny, theft, fraud, or forgery, (B) money laundering or (C) tax evasion.

I certify that I have not been convicted within the last 10 years of any one of the following in connection with a mortgage or real estate transaction:

      (a) felony larceny, theft, fraud, or forgery,
      (b) money laundering or
      (c) tax evasion.

I understand that the servicer of the mortgage loan secured by the Property (the Servicer), the U.S. Department of the Treasury (Treasury), or their respective agents may investigate the accuracy of my statements by performing routine background checks, including automated searches of federal, state and county databases, to confirm that I have not been convicted of such crimes. I also understand that knowingly submitting false information may violate Federal law. This certification is effective on the earlier of the date listed below or the date this form is received by the Servicer.

ACKNOWLEDGEMENT AND AGREEMENT

1. I authorize and give permission to the Servicer, Treasury, and their respective agents, to assemble and use a current consumer report to investigate my eligibility for HAFA relocation assistance, the accuracy of my statements and any documentation that I may provide in connection with requesting HAFA relocation assistance. I understand that these consumer reports may include, without limitation, a credit report, and be assembled and used at any point to assess my eligibility.

2. I understand that if I have engaged in fraud or if it is determined that any of my statements or any information contained in the documentation that I provide are materially false and that I was ineligible for relocation assistance under HAFA, the Servicer, Treasury, or their respective agents may seek remedies available at law and in equity, such as recouping any assistance I previously received.

3. I understand that the Servicer will collect and record personal information that I submit, including, but not limited to, my name, address, social security number and date of birth. I understand and consent to the Servicer's disclosure of my personal information and the terms of any assistance I may receive under MHA to Treasury and its agents, Fannie Mae and Freddie Mac in connection with their responsibilities under MHA, companies that perform support services in conjunction with MHA, any investor, insurer, guarantor, or servicer that owns, insures, guarantees, or services the mortgage loan(s) secured by the Property, and to any HUD-certified housing counselor assisting Owner.

4. I understand that the Owner may, but is not required to, request relocation assistance on my behalf. I authorize the Owner to submit this Certification to the Servicer in connection with any such request, along with any other documentation that the Servicer may require, and I authorize the Servicer to disclose to the Owner the results of any inquiry completed in conjunction with said Certifications and documentation.

The undersigned certifies under penalty of perjury that all statements in this document are true and correct.

| Occupant Signature | Social Security Number | Date of Birth | Date |

| Co-Occupant Signature | Social Security Number | Date of Birth | Date |

Page 1 of 2

NOTICE TO OCCUPANTS

Be advised that by signing this document you understand that any documents and information you submit in connection with the Making Home Affordable Program are under penalty of perjury. Any misstatement of material fact made in the completion of these documents including but not limited to misstatement regarding your occupancy in the Property, will subject you to potential criminal investigation and prosecution for the following crimes: perjury, false statements, mail fraud, and wire fraud. The information contained in these documents is subject to examination and verification. Any potential misrepresentation will be referred to the appropriate law enforcement authority for investigation and prosecution. By signing this document you certify, represent and agree that: "Under penalty of perjury, all documents and information I have provided in connection with the Making Home Affordable Program, including the documents and information regarding my eligibility for relocation assistance under HAFA, are true and correct."

If you are aware of fraud, waste, abuse, mismanagement or misrepresentations affiliated with the Troubled Asset Relief Program, please contact the SIGTARP Hotline by calling 1-877-SIG-2009 (toll-free), 202-622-4559 (fax), or www.sigtarp.gov and provide them with your name, the Owner's name, the property address and reason for escalation. Mail can be sent to Hotline Office of the Special Inspector General for Troubled Asset Relief Program, 1801 L St. NW, Washington, DC 20220.

MAKING HOME AFFORDABLE PROGRAMS

- **Home Affordable Foreclosure Alternatives Program** (HAFA)

  http://www.makinghomeaffordable.gov/programs/exit-gracefully/Pages/hafa.aspx

- **Home Affordable Modification Program** (HAMP)

  http://www.makinghomeaffordable.gov/programs/lower-payments/Pages/hamp.aspx

- **Principal Reduction Alternative** (PRA)

  http://www.makinghomeaffordable.gov/programs/lower-payments/Pages/pra.aspx

- **Second Lien Modification Program** (2MP)

  http://www.makinghomeaffordable.gov/programs/second-mortgage-help/Pages/default.aspx

- **Home Affordable Unemployment Program** (UP)

  http://www.makinghomeaffordable.gov/programs/unemployed-help/Pages/up.aspx

- **Home Affordable Refinance Program** (HARP)

  http://www.makinghomeaffordable.gov/programs/lower-rates/Pages/harp.aspx

- Housing Finance Agency Fund for the Hardest Hit Housing Markets (HHF)

  http://www.makinghomeaffordable.gov/programs/unemployed-help/Pages/hhf.aspx

- FHA Home Affordable Modification Program (FHA-HAMP)

  http://www.makinghomeaffordable.gov/programs/lower-payments/Pages/fha-hamp.aspx

- Second Lien Modification Program for FHA Loans (FHA-2LP)

  http://www.makinghomeaffordable.gov/programs/lower-rates/Pages/fha2lp.aspx

- FHA Refinance for Borrowers with Negative Equity (FHA Short Refinance)

  http://www.makinghomeaffordable.gov/programs/lower-rates/Pages/short-refinance.aspx

- USDA's Special Loan Servicing

  http://www.makinghomeaffordable.gov/programs/lower-payments/Pages/rd-hamp.aspx

- Veteran's Affairs Home Affordable Modification (VA-HAMP)

  http://www.makinghomeaffordable.gov/programs/lower-payments/Pages/va-hamp.aspx

SCAM AVOIDANCE

MAKING HOME AFFORDABLE STATEMENT[12]

Beware of Foreclosure Rescue Scams!

Real Help is Free!

Foreclosure rescue and mortgage modification scams are a growing problem that could cost you thousands of dollars – or even your home.

Scammers make promises that they can't keep, such as guaranteeing to "save" your home or lower your mortgage, usually for a fee, often pretending that they have direct contact with your mortgage servicer – which they do not.

But the federal government provides the help you need for free!

Just call 888-995-HOPE (4673) for information about The Making Home Affordable Program ® and to speak with a HUD-approved housing counselor. Assistance is available free, 24-7, in 160 languages.

Tips to Avoid Scams:

1. Beware of anyone who asks you to pay a fee in exchange for counseling services or the modification of a delinquent loan.
2. Beware of people who pressure you to sign papers immediately or who try to convince you that they can "save" your home if you sign or transfer over the deed to your house.
3. Do not sign over the deed to your property to any organization or individual unless you are working directly with your mortgage company to forgive your debt.
4. Never make a mortgage payment to anyone other than your mortgage company without their approval.

What to Do if You Have Been the Victim of a Scam

If you believe you have been the victim of a scam, you should file a complaint with the Federal Trade Commission (FTC). Visit the FTC's online Complaint Assistant or call 877-FTC-HELP (877-382-4357) for assistance in English or Spanish.

---

[12] http://www.makinghomeaffordable.gov/learning-center/Pages/beware.aspx

STOPFRAUD.GOV STATEMENT[13]

To Report Mortgage Fraud or Loan Scams:

Federal Bureau of Investigation
Phone: 1-800-CALLFBI (225-5324)
Online Tips: FBI Tips and Public Leads Form
To file a complaint with the FBI contact the nearest FBI field office. Locations are listed at www.fbi.gov/contactus.htm or https://tips.fbi.gov/ or for major cases, you can also report information by calling toll-free number 1-800-CALLFBI (225-5324).

Housing and Urban Development (HUD) Office of the Inspector General Hotline
Phone: (800) 347-3735
Fax: (202) 708-4829
Email: hotline@hudoig.gov
Address: HUD OIG Hotline (GFI), 451 7th Street, SW, Washington, DC 20410

PreventLoanScams.org: A project of the Lawyers' Committee for Civil Rights Under the Law
Website: PreventLoanScams.org
Phone: 1-888-995-HOPE
PreventLoanScams.org - was launched to serve as a nationwide clearinghouse for loan modification scam information on complaints filed, laws and regulations, and enforcement actions. If you think you've been scammed or approached by a company or individual promising to help you with your foreclosure, report it today.

Federal Trade Commission (FTC): Complaint Assistant
Web Site (Spanish): https://www.ftccomplaintassistant.gov/Consumer_HomeES.htm
Phone (for complaints against companies, organizations, or business practices): (877) FTC-HELP
Phone (for complaints about identity theft): (877) ID-THEFT
Email Address (for complaints about spam or phishing): spam@uce.gov
The Federal Trade Commission collects complaints about fraud, companies, business practices, identity theft, and episodes of violence in the media.

---

[13] http://www.stopfraud.gov/report.html#mortgage

Glossary of Terms[14]

Acceleration. A loan in default may be called due, the first step in a foreclosure, regardless of its actual due date. Correcting the default, which can be accomplished by loan modification, ends the threat.

Adjustable Rate Mortgage. Some loans are designed with an interest rate that changes from time to time. The periodic changes are determined by adding a fixed margin to a variable index rate, which reflects market conditions and allows lenders to maintain a current yield. Changes may be limited by lifetime and period caps, which may be maximums or minimums. All elements – index, margin, caps, and period – are defined in the promissory note.

Affidavit. A written statement, which affirms that its contents are true and accurate.

Agreement Not to Foreclose. Temporarily suspends or delays foreclosure proceedings when a condition of default exists. Typically, an unwritten temporary suspension during a pending modification. A formal proposal would be strengthened by evidence of disclosure or loan closing document irregularities, or predatory lending practices.

Amortization. When loan payments include both interest and principal, each payment reduces the outstanding loan balance. As the loan balance declines, less of the payment goes to interest and more goes to principal, thus accelerating the reduction of the loan balance over time. If paid completely, the loan is fully amortizing.

---

[14] The following descriptions and explanations are offered by the author for quick reference in context of this book. They have no legal significance. Before relying on any definition, ensure that it is correct in the context and jurisdiction where used.

Balloon Payment. When a loan is not fully amortizing, a principal balance remains at the end of the loan term, and is due in a lump-sum payment. See Amortization.

Bankruptcy. Forgiveness of debt through a judicial process. When bankruptcy is a consideration, its procedures and consequences should always be discussed with qualified legal counsel and financial advisors.

Capitalized Principal Balance. Includes the unpaid principal balance (UPB) of a loan, plus payments advanced by the lender for such expenses as property tax or insurance not paid by a borrower. It might also include the interest portion of missed payments, but must exclude late fees or administrative costs if a modification occurs.

Cash Reserves. Also known as liquid assets, money that can be withdrawn within a short period of time. Obvious are checking and savings accounts. Others are sellable stocks, bonds, mutual funds, money market funds, and, for HAMP purposes, certificates of deposit of any maturity. Excluded are retirement accounts, whether self-administered (IRA, 401k, Keogh, etc.) or other-administered (employer, pension), and deferred compensation or stock options. See also Emergency Reserve.

CheckMyNPV.com. Web-based self-service tool for borrowers and their advisors to independently predict potential NPV eligibility for HAMP. Go to https://checkmynpv.com/

Claim Advance. If the mortgage is insured, the insurer may consider an interest-free loan to bring the account current, avoiding a lender's claim for a loss from foreclosure or short sale. Full repayment of the interim loan might be delayed for several years.

Combined Loan-to-Value Ratio (CLTV). Calculated by dividing the total combined senior and junior loan amounts by the property value. See Loan-to-Value Ratio.

Current Monthly Mortgage Payment. The mortgage payment including property tax and insurance prior to modification. See Mortgage Payment.

Current Monthly P&I. Shorthand for "principal and interest." See Monthly P&I.

Debt. As used to calculate the debt coverage ratio, the current principal and interest portion of the current monthly mortgage payment for the loan to be modified.

Debt Coverage Ratio. The relationship of net income to loan payments, indicating the income "cushion" that remains after making those payments. Used in the Fannie Mae and other imminent default screens.

Debt-to-Income Ratio. See Gross Expense-to-Income Ratio.

Deed-in-Lieu of Foreclosure. Often simply called "deed-in-lieu." Borrower voluntarily surrenders ownership of the property to lender, and the debt is forgiven. This option may be unavailable if other liens encumber title to the property (for example, judgments of other creditors, junior mortgages, IRS or state tax liens). Sometimes referred colloquially as "turning over the keys."

Deed of Trust. Also known as a trust deed, a form of mortgage that allows for enforcement of the lender's claim according to a pre-defined and streamlined procedure sanctioned by State law. In a foreclosure, the trust deed allows a lender (through a trustee) to sell the underlying property without judicial action, but then precludes recourse to borrower's other assets. See Single Action Rule.

Deficiency Judgment. When a loan is not paid in full, a deficiency results. If the lender sues the borrower for the deficit amount and wins, then the court enters a deficiency judgment, which may be enforced as any other award of the court. See Single Action Rule.

Disposable Net Income. Income left after payroll deductions, all credit obligations, including housing and living expenses, but excluding the mortgage payment to be modified.

Eligibility. Borrower, mortgage, property, and lender must meet a set of criteria before a loan may be considered for modification under HAMP.

Emergency Reserve. Equal to three times monthly "debt payments," according to HAMP. Fannie Mae limits the reserve to three times monthly "housing expenses," which is a lower cash reserve amount. See also Cash Reserve.

Equity. The difference between the value of property and the encumbrances, liens, loans, and other claims against the property. This net value is the ownership interest in the property. If it is a negative amount, the terms "negative equity" and "underwater" are commonly used.

Escalation. The process used by a borrower or advisor to challenge and correct a lender's negative decision.

Escrow. A disinterested third party is appointed to hold items of value deposited by one party with instructions to deliver those items to another party on the occurrence of a predetermined event. An example is the sale and purchase of a home. The seller deposits a conveyance deed and the buyer deposits (or arranges for a lender to deposit) funds equaling the purchase price. Each instructs escrow to deliver the deposited items to the other when all the conditions of the sale and purchase are complete.

Escrow Account. An accumulating amount paid by a borrower monthly and held by the lender to pay annual or semi-annual property tax and insurance premium payments. Sometimes referred to as an impound account.

Estimated Principal Balance. The loan amount used to determine the modified payments. Includes the balance at time of modification, plus past due interest and escrow amounts paid by the lender on behalf of the borrower. It may not include late fees and other administrative costs. See Capitalized Principal Balance.

Fannie Mae. Founded in 1938, one of two Government Sponsored Enterprises used to underwrite trillions of dollars of mortgages, allowing the private financial markets to fund the American Dream of homeownership. After suffering substantial losses due to deteriorated real estate and mortgage markets, placed into conservatorship in September 2008 under the Federal Housing Finance Agency. See also Freddie Mac.

Federal Housing Finance Agency. Conservator for Fannie Mae and Freddie Mac.

Forbearance. A reduction or suspension of payments with lender's agreement, while negotiating another form of relief or until a temporary difficulty ends.

Forbearance of Interest. A waiver of interest on a portion of the loan principal to reduce monthly payments to an affordable and sustainable level. That portion of principal must be repaid, but without interest.

Foreclosure. A statutory procedure beginning with a borrower's default in payments on a loan, and ending with the sale of the property securing the loan. The sale proceeds go first to paying the costs of sale, then to paying the loan. If the proceeds are insufficient to satisfy the loan, State law determines whether the borrower may be held personally liable. See Judicial Foreclosure, Single Action Rule, and Trustee Sale.

Foreclosure Alternatives. Includes modification, principal forgiveness and forbearance, short sale and deed-in-lieu of foreclosure within the Making Home Affordable program. Refer to Appendix 10, *Making Home Affordable Programs*, page 91. Usually also available as proprietary programs at individual servicers.

Forgiveness. A permanent reduction of the unpaid principal balance (UPB) of a loan. See Principal Forgiveness.

Freddie Mac. Founded in 1970, one of two Government Sponsored Enterprises used to underwrite trillions of dollars of mortgages, allowing the private financial markets to bankroll the American Dream of homeowners. In September 2008, after suffering substantial losses due to deteriorated real estate and mortgage markets, placed into conservatorship under the Federal Housing Finance Agency. See also Fannie Mae.

Government Sponsored Enterprises (GSE). See Fannie Mae and Freddie Mac.

Gross Expense-to-Income Ratio. Compares income from all sources with all credit and most living expenses, and measures relative debt burden, overall ability to meet obligations, viability of the loan modification beyond its impact on monthly mortgage payments, and responsible use of borrowed money. Also referred to as the "monthly debt ratio," "debt-to-income ratio," and "'back-end' ratio."

Gross Income. All income from any source, before withholding or deductions, including earnings received from self-employment and non-employment sources such as pension or public assistance. A component of the monthly mortgage payment ratio.

Homeowner Association (HOA). The governing board for a condominium. planned unit development (PUD), or other group of homeowners gathered for a common purpose. Fees are collected from homeowners for administering the group and improving, maintaining, and repairing the property. Unpaid fees may become a lien against the individual owner's property.

Hardship Affidavit. A standardized form for describing the "events" that contribute to a borrower's difficulty making mortgage payments. A central component of eligibility, a borrower must the Hardship events in writing.

Housing Expense. Occasionally used with the same meaning as monthly mortgage payment. See Mortgage Payment.

Imminent Risk of Default. The likelihood that a borrower, who is current on payments, will be unable to continue making timely payments. Either the lender must find a borrower to be "at risk," or a borrower must be 60 or more days late (seriously delinquent), to be eligible for modification. Also referred to as "reasonably foreseeable default."

Impound Account. See Escrow Account.

Income. See Gross Income.

Initial Package. Begins the HAMP evaluation process. It consists of the Request for Mortgage Assistance (RMA) form, IRS form 4506-T or 4506T-EZ, and evidence of income.

Interest Rate Cap. The Freddie Mac 30-year fixed rate at the time of the modification determines the maximum rate for the modified loan.

Investor. In this book, "investor" refers to the actual owner of a mortgage, which is the right to receive repayment of the loan amount and interest on outstanding principal. In the past, the financial institution lending the money was also the investor, on behalf of its depositors. Recently, money has been raised in financial markets through mortgage-backed securities (securities backed by a pool of similar mortgages), and the issuer of the securities is now the investor. See Loan Servicer.

Judicial Foreclosure. An action in court to enforce a lender's secured interest in real estate. In effect, it is a lawsuit for breach of contract when a borrower defaults on the promissory note. A costly and time-consuming alternative, it is seldom used when the mortgage includes a separate enforcement provision, as in a deed of trust.

Lender. In this book, "lender" refers generically to the originator, servicer, and/or investor of the mortgage. Specifically, it refers to the recipient of a borrower's monthly payments and request for modification.

Lien. A claim against property, typically to ensure repayment of a debt, but also to ensure payment for certain services to improve the property (for example, "mechanics lien" for construction, repairs, and materials) or to ensure payment of charges against the property (for example, "tax lien" for unpaid property taxes).

Loan Servicer. See Servicer. See also Lender; used interchangeably in this book.

Loan-to-Value Ratio (LTV). Calculated by dividing the senior loan amount by the property value. The lower the result, the less risk to a lender and the more equity vested in the owner. Any result greater than 100%, however, is commonly referred to as "negative equity" or being "underwater."

Modification Agreement. The agreement between a lender and a borrower that permanently changes the promissory note. It becomes effective upon completion of the trial period.

Modification Evaluator. A tool to help borrowers determine whether they might be eligible for a Home Affordable Modification. Go to http://makinghomeaffordable.gov/evaluator.html.

Monthly Debt Ratio. See Gross Expense-to-Income Ratio.

Monthly Disposable Net Income. Income left after payroll deductions, all credit obligations, including housing and living expenses, but excluding the mortgage payment to be modified. See Disposable Net Income.

Monthly Gross Expenses. Though HAMP identifies specific expense items, generally includes mortgage payments, other housing expenses, and credit obligations.

Monthly Gross Income. See Gross Income.

Monthly Mortgage Payment. See Mortgage Payment.

Monthly Mortgage Payment Ratio. See Mortgage Payment Ratio.

Monthly Obligations. Include personal debts, revolving (credit card) accounts, installment loans, and household or living expenses.

Monthly P&I. The principal and interest payment that traditionally has been considered the "mortgage payment." However, for HAMP purposes, P&I is a component of the monthly mortgage payment, which also include escrow account payments. See Amortization. Contrast Negative Amortization and interest-only payments.

Mortgage. A lien or claim against real property (real estate) to ensure repayment of a loan, almost always for the purpose of buying the property, refinancing a previous loan, or liquidating equity accumulated from a down payment or value appreciation. The borrower owns the real estate, but the lender has a claim or interest in the real estate, specifically the right to sell it and collect what is owed from the sale proceeds if the borrower does not repay the loan as agreed. The term "mortgage" usually refers to both the loan agreement (promissory note) and the security instrument (mortgage or deed of trust).

Mortgage Payment. Combines the principal and interest paid to the lender, plus monthly allotments for property taxes and insurance, HOA fees, and certain other assessments. It does not include the payment for any second mortgage or for mortgage insurance, which are included in debt and in monthly obligations. Also see Target Monthly Mortgage Payment.

Mortgage Payment Ratio. Calculates the portion of income needed to pay housing expenses by dividing the monthly mortgage payment by gross monthly income. It is commonly referred to as the "housing-to-income" or "front-end" ratio. See Target Monthly Mortgage Payment Ratio.

Negative Equity. See Equity. Also known as "underwater."

Negative Amortization. When loan payments are less than interest owed, and the unpaid interest is added to the loan balance, the balance increases. This is opposite or negative compared to amortization, which reduces the loan balance.

Net Income. See Disposable Net Income.

Net Present Value (NPV). The current value of future costs and benefits (cash flow) to a lender from modifying a mortgage versus foreclosing on it.

NPV Input Values. Individual credit, property, loan and similar unique variables used when evaluating a borrower in the NPV Test.

NPV Test. The process of determining the net present value of a loan, and comparing the results. If modification is more beneficial to the lender than foreclosure, then the results are "positive" and the lender is required by HAMP to modify. Otherwise, the lender may modify or not, but should consider foreclosure alternatives.

Non-Approval. Denial by a lender of a request for modification due to borrower's ineligibility or negative NPV Test findings, sometimes for failure to arrive at a viable monthly mortgage payment using the standard modification waterfall.

Non-Approval Notice. Written explanation to the borrower from the lender that lists the reasons for the denying a request for modification.

Non-Recourse Agreement. Lender agrees not to make claims against assets of a borrower other than the property to compensate for any deficiency. Might be imposed by statute.

Payment Constant. A number that corresponds to an interest rate and amortization term. The fully amortizing payment for any loan amount, at that rate and term, can be found by multiplying the loan amount by the Payment Constant.

Payment Reduction Estimator. A tool available to help an eligible borrower estimate the payment resulting from a modification. Go to http://makinghomeaffordable.gov/payment_reduction_estimator.html.

Pooling and Servicing Agreement. Governs the relationship between a loan servicer and investor. It may restrict loan servicers in applying HAMP to modify loans, even if the servicer has entered a Servicer Participant Agreement.

Pre-Foreclosure Sale. See Short Sale.

Principal Balance. The amount of a loan that remains unpaid. Same as unpaid principal balance (UPB).

Principal Forbearance. A portion of the loan on which monthly payments are not required and interest is not charged (non-interest bearing). Intended to further reduce the modified monthly mortgage payment. The amount must be paid as a balloon payment when the loan is due. Contrast Principal Forgiveness.

Principal Forgiveness. An actual reduction of the outstanding loan amount. Not due in the future. Also, effectively reduces the monthly payment.

Promissory Note. The agreement or contract that defines the terms and conditions of a loan and its repayment. A Promissory Note for a real estate loan should always be secured by a mortgage or deed of trust, which serves to enforce the promise to repay.

Proposed Principal Balance. A tactic suggested in this book to reduce the estimated (capitalized) principal balance on which modified payments are calculated. It would require principal forgiveness by the lender.

Qualification. In this book, refers to the credit analysis or underwriting of a borrower's ability to make modified loan payments. Contrast with "eligibility," which involves a set of threshold criteria.

Reasonably Foreseeable Default. See Imminent Risk of Default.

Re-Default. After modifying a delinquent loan, the borrower misses the modified payments and again becomes delinquent.

Reinstatement. Pay by a specific date all back interest and principal owed, in exchange for "reinstating" the loan to its pre-default status. Will take the loan out of delinquency status, but will not reverse previous delinquency reports to credit bureaus. Typically combined with forbearance and the expectation of a windfall (e.g. bonus, investment, insurance settlement, tax refund).

Repayment Plan. An agreement between lender and borrower that apportions delinquent amounts to subsequent payments until all back interest, late fees, and other included amounts are paid. Results in a temporary or permanent increase in payments. May also be used to repay a forbearance amount. See Forbearance.

Request for Modification and Affidavit (RMA). Former name of Request for Mortgage Assistance.

Request for Mortgage Assistance (RMA). Principal form in the Initial Package to commence consideration for Making Home Affordable mortgage relief.

Requestor. The borrower or authorized third party who escalates a disputed case.

Servicer. Collects payments as the investor's agent, keeping its fees, and then passing-through the remainder. In this book, also referred to as "lender."

Servicer Participant Agreement (SPA). The agreement entered by loan servicers and lenders that participate in HAMP. In return for complying with HAMP guidelines, they are entitled to receive incentive payments from the federal government.

Short Payoff. Lender agrees to accept less than the full amount owed and the difference (shortfall) is forgiven, usually resulting in a lower loss to lender than foreclosure.

Short Refinance. Refinancing to a more affordable mortgage by a qualified borrower that results in a short payoff, often due to decline in property value. Has the effect of a principal reduction, and is unusual. Complicated by any junior lien or judgment.

Short Sale. A conventional sale when the net proceeds are less than the loan balance, resulting in a short payoff. Lender agrees to accept less than the full amount owed, releases the lien (security interest) so title may pass unencumbered to the buyer, and might waive (forgive) the unpaid portion of the loan principal (deficiency or shortfall).

Single Action Rule. In some states, a lender must choose to foreclose based on the security instrument (mortgage or deed of trust) or sue for breach of contract (promissory note), but not both. In almost every instance, residential lenders will foreclose, thereby eliminating a lawsuit and a deficiency judgment.

Single Family Property. Any residential real estate with one-to-four units. In MHA language, it is not limited to a single dwelling structure.

Standard Modification Waterfall. The sequence of steps required by HAMP to reduce the interest rate, extend the amortization term, and forbear principal as needed to arrive at a mortgage payment that is "affordable and sustainable" for the homeowner.

Target Monthly Mortgage Payment. The modified payment calculated by multiplying gross monthly income by the target monthly mortgage payment ratio, which may not be less than 31%. The payment totals the reduced principal and interest payment, plus the other listed expenses.

Target Monthly Mortgage Payment Ratio. The objective is to reduce the payment until this Ratio closely approaches, but does not fall below 31%. To determine the target monthly mortgage payment, multiply gross monthly income by the 31% and round up when applying the modified interest rate, amortization, and principal forbearance.

Trial Period. Precedes the actual loan modification. Typically lasts three months and involves a trial period plan and preparation of the final modification agreement.

Trial Period Plan. Defines the terms of a trial period, primarily modified payments and due dates. Modification requires completion of the trial period according to the Plan.

Trust Deed. See Deed of Trust.

Trustee Sale. The foreclosure sale under a deed of trust. Also known as a non-judicial foreclosure, because it requires no further legal or judicial action for its enforcement.

Underwriting. The process of analyzing the ability to repay and creditworthiness of an applicant for a loan or other extension or modification of credit.

Unpaid Principal Balance (UPB). The unpaid portion of a loan. Same as principal balance.

Dean Allen Kackley is a licensed attorney and real estate broker with a thorough knowledge of the federal Making Home Affordable Modification Program. He counsels borrowers regarding mortgage relief options and represents them in loan workouts with their lenders. In addition to a wide variety of real estate transactions, his lending experience spans more than two decades.

After joining Wells Fargo Bank in 1985, then a "portfolio" lender that owned all loans originated, Kackley helped to develop its residential mortgage business with his broad knowledge of underwriting, settlement, and servicing functions. He worked briefly for the Independent National Mortgage Corporation (IndyMac), a market-maker for mortgage-backed securities (MBS), mortgage pooling and servicing investments, and alternate and sub-prime loans.

In more than $250 million of sale, lease, and financing transactions, his experience involves residential, commercial, and land development properties, and hundreds of closings. A graduate of Yale University and the University of Kansas School of Law, Dean Kackley writes with a passion, intelligence, understanding, and clarity that are rare for this kind of book. His practice is located in Napa Valley, California.

Description of the Book

Mortgage problems? This book will help. It is the consumer's version of new federal rules for short sales for homeowners and landlords with underwater mortgages. It's the most current and important information available for owners in distress.

Professional advisors can benefit in two important ways, especially real estate agents and brokers. This quick guide helps you master the wide-reaching changes effective June 1, 2012. It also helps your prospects and clients to become better informed, to assist not resist.

Rely on this valuable resource during a grueling, but necessary process. It can shift the balance of power and help you get control. Cut through technical jargon and specialized knowledge. Homeowners and landlords, and their trusted advisors now have a simple, quick, and complete reference when working with lenders.

It covers everything you need to know and do to successfully complete a HAFA short sale ... the federal Making Home Affordable Foreclosure Alternatives program ... and to work effectively with Bank of America, Chase, Wells Fargo, CitiMortgage, GMAC/Ally, and other participating servicers.

This is the quickest guide to short sales for homeowners, landlords, and their professional advisors. Level the playing field and get the results you want.

www.ingramcontent.com/pod-product-compliance
Lightning Source LLC
Chambersburg PA
CBHW072308290526
45794CB00002B/578